Preaching According to the Holy Spirit

Jay E. Adams

TIMELESS TEXTS
Woodruff, SC

Contents

Introduction

In chapter eight of his *Autobiography*, Benjamin Franklin wrote:

Tho' I seldom attended any public worship, I had still an opinion of its propriety, and of its utility when rightly conducted, and I regularly paid my annual subscription for the support of the only Presbyterian minister or meeting we had in Philadelphia. He used to visit me sometimes as a friend, and admonish me to attend his administrations, and I was now and then prevailed upon to do so, once for five Sundays successively. Had he been in my opinion a good preacher, perhaps I might have continued, notwithstanding the occasion I had for the Sunday's leisure in my course of study; but his discourses were chiefly either polemic arguments, or explications of the peculiar doctrines of our sect, and were all to me very dry, uninteresting, and unedifying, since not a single moral principle was inculcated or enforced, their aim seeming to be rather to make us Presbyterians than good citizens.

At length, he took for his text that verse of the fourth chapter of Philippians, "Finally, brethren, whatsoever things are true, honest, just, pure, lovely, or of good report, if there be any virtue, or any praise, think on these things." And I imagined, in a sermon on such a text, we could not miss having some morality. But he confined himself to five points only, as meant by the apostle, viz: 1. Keeping holy the Sabbath day. 2. Being diligent in reading the holy Scriptures. 3. Attending duly the public worship. 4. Partaking of the Sacrament. 5. Paying due respect to

God's ministers. These might be all good things; but, as they were not the kind of good things I had expected from that text, I despaired of ever meeting with them from any other, was disgusted, and attended his preaching no more.

Shame on that Presbyterian preacher! While due consideration of the unregenerate condition of Franklin leading to his neglect of the church and the possibility of excuse making must be given; nevertheless, from his description of the situation one can glean enough information to conclude that his preacher missed a golden opportunity. And—note the fact—it was his shoddy preaching that drove Franklin away. If it was his desire to hear only morality rather than doctrine that "disgusted" him, one might make allowances for the unregenerate mind. But clearly, it seems that it was more than that. The preacher simply didn't know how to preach. It sounds like he was a poor exegete who missed the point of the text and who was bent on lecturing people rather then preaching to them. Franklin's assessment doesn't seem too far off the mark.

All too often, men who have heard academic lecturing from grade school through seminary have learned only to replicate the sort of thing that they sat under for so many years. They are apt at arguing doctrine, mouthing familiar truisms, and boring people to death with truth academically presented. They can give stuffy lectures, but they don't know how to preach! The Word of the living God is not boring. It is not irrelevant. It is only poor preachers who make it seem so. That is a travesty that must be remedied. And it is about time for the ministers of the church of Jesus Christ to rise up and demand something more of their seminary professors! This book is one attempt to do something about the problem.

Since the Bible itself is filled with wonderful examples of powerful and interesting preaching, it is only right that preachers should be taught how this preaching that "turned the world upside down" was done. But instead of studying the apostolic preachers who, against all odds, succeeded in spreading the Word of the Lord throughout the then known world, homileticians spend their time inculcating the tired principles of ancient Greek and Roman rhetoric and the modern tenets of communication theory that are overloaded with jargon and light on substance. Why don't they carefully learn and teach what they can from the Bible itself?

Too often the homileticians do little more than repeat the dictums of the homileticians who taught them. These men, in turn, did the same thing—a practice that has been going on for nearly two thousand years. Bad preaching has been the result—the inevitable effect of their (however well-meaning) neglecting the true Source from which to glean the help that is needed for preaching God's Word as He would have it preached.

I am not saying that God has not used mediocre and even poor preaching to bring men to faith in Christ or to build up the saints in their most holy faith. But when He does this, it is not because of the preaching by which Scriptural truth is conveyed, but in spite of it. God may bless His Word even in the worst cases, but that fact doesn't relieve the preacher from his responsibility to "adorn" the doctrine of God. Where God succeeds, the poor preacher fails. The issue is not God's power to bless but the preacher's power to harm!

There are many books about preaching on the shelves of the seminary libraries. I have over three hundred in my own personal library alone. There are courses of instruction in preaching at every seminary worth its salt. But in spite of these facts, there is a plethora of poor preachers. For years I taught preaching in two theological seminaries. I read everything that I could get my hands on. But I was appalled at the meager help that the hundreds of books I surveyed had to offer. Again and again there were the same flat platitudes, tired truisms and old saws that homileticians had been passing along for years. I was disgusted to find very little fresh or important in them. But most of all, I discovered that the authors thought it unnecessary to turn to the Scriptures in any serious way to discover what is and is not important to know about preaching. Out there in the homiletic world, as most preachers will tell you from their own experience, there is virtually no exegetical effort made to understand what preaching should be like. Homiletic professors have been notoriously weak in the languages. Most don't even do exegesis in their texts. One wonders what they teach in the classroom. What attempts a few have made in this direction have been largely superficial and the results desultory. They simply have turned everywhere else for help instead of to the Bible itself. That is strange—very strange—since it is the preachers in the Scriptures who ought to be our models and who, you would think, ought to have the most to say about what preaching should be. Strange, I say, but true. Look high and low and far and wide and you will find precious little of an exegetical or biblical nature in the study of preaching.

I hope in part at least, to attempt to remedy the situation. This book is the fruit of many years of study in which I have tried to understand what the Bible has to say about preaching. Doubtless, I have not written the last word. But perhaps, in a genuine sense, I may have written the first one. That is to say, I believe that I am breaking new ground here. I hope that others will catch the vision that I have set forth as well as profit from the helpful materials that I have amassed. I hope that in time some may refine and amplify what I have presented in this more-or-less pristine form. My desire is to see an up-and-coming line of new preachers who will benefit from these kinds of books and afford to the Benjamin Franklins of their day no excuses for neglecting the ministry of the Word.

In this book I shall examine the Holy Spirit's concerns about preaching in an effort to make them equally yours. "The Holy Spirit's concerns?" you ask, "Where can you find those? Surely, you aren't advocating some sort of extra-biblical revelation, are you?" If you have read my book *The Christian's Guide to Guidance,* you would know that I consider any such thing anathema. "How, then, do you claim access to the Spirit's concerns about preaching?" As you will see in the next chapter, I shall do so by careful exegesis of the New Testament on the matter. As I said, so little homiletic work has been in the biblical documents themselves that I am not surprised at your puzzlement.

Chapter 1

Apostolic Preaching Was Unique

"Yes, it was. So, then, why look to it as a model? Our preaching isn't unique."

Ah, but you miss the point.

"How so?"

The very fact that it is unique is what makes it valuable for you and me.

"I'm afraid that I don't get it; you'd better explain."

Delighted. Here's the scoop: The apostolic preaching was unique in that it was *inspired*.

"What? I've never heard that before. And if it's true, then isn't that worse? Doesn't that make it even *less* of a model for us? After all, our preaching isn't inspired."

Again, you miss the point. If their preaching was inspired—and I shall show you that it was—then, by it, we have been given the supreme model for preaching. In it we can see what the Holy Spirit, Who inspired the apostles, considers important, what He approves, and how He expects preaching to be carried on.

"Well, that *sounds* reasonable. Have at it! I'll let you know if I'm convinced."

Good. We shall begin by looking at what Jesus said apostolic preaching would be like. He predicted the fact of inspiration on at least two occasions.

In the following verses, the Lord Jesus Christ promised to send the Holy Spirit to inspire the preaching of the apostles. As you read through each verse, try to determine what it was that He said the Holy Spirit would do to help them preach effectively. When you can list these promises (and I suggest that a careful reading will reveal four main promises), you will have a list of the *concerns* that the Holy Spirit has for preaching. If you can identify these concerns, you will then be able to make those same concerns your *own* concerns in preaching so that, when you prepare and deliver messages, you too will be focusing on the things that the Holy Spirit thinks are crucial to good preaching. Then more and more you will find yourself *Preaching According to the Holy Spirit*. Could anything be more important for a preacher to know than what God thinks is important about preaching? Isn't it crucial to understand what the Spirit considers essential? Wouldn't it have been important to have learned that in seminary before you ever went out to preach? How much more valuable to know God's requirements for good preaching rather than those of some homiletician—no matter how wise he may be!

Of course, it is never too late to learn. It is always of use to discover these things at any time in one's ministry. If you are a seasoned preacher, who is dedicated to pleasing the Lord by his preaching, you too will want to compare where you put the emphasis in your preparation and delivery with where the Spirit does. Do these emphases correspond, or do they differ? If the former, great! Continue to do as you have been doing. Indeed, do so with greater confidence that you are on the right track. If the latter, then you will have to make adjustments. You may have to de-emphasize certain matters, place much more emphasis on others, or even abandon certain practices altogether. Do you see now what I am up to in this book? If so, let's go on.

Here are the principal verses that we need to study at first:

> But when they deliver you up, don't worry about what you will say or how you will say it, because what you must say will be given to you in that hour. You aren't the ones who will be speaking, but the Spirit of My Father speaking in you.
>
> (Matthew 10:19, 20)

Now when they arrest you and bring you to trial, don't worry beforehand about what you will say. Rather, say whatever is given to you in that hour (it won't be you speaking, but the Holy Spirit).
(Mark 13:11)

Now, when they bring you before synagogs and rulers and authorities, don't worry about what you will say in defense or how to do so because the Holy Spirit will teach you in that very hour what you ought to say.   (Luke 12:11, 12)

Get it settled in your hearts not to practice your defense beforehand, because I will give you words[1] and wisdom that none of your opponents will be able to withstand or contradict.
(Luke 21:14, 15)

As I said, these are the key passages that we shall be looking at in this chapter and upon which much of those chapters that follow also depend. They are passages that you rarely, if ever, encounter in the preaching textbooks, so we shall find it necessary to spend some time analyzing them. The homileticians, it seems, haven't even thought about the relevance of Christ's promises to the preaching of the apostles.

To begin with, then, let us note that the Lord Jesus said that the apostles would not **be the ones speaking, but the Spirit of** His **Father speaking in them.** In similar words He declared **it won't be** [they] **speaking, but the Holy Spirit.** Moreover, He promised **the Holy Spirit** [would] **teach** [them] **in that very hour what** [they] **ought to say**, and assured them that He would

---

[1] Literally, "a mouth." The idea here is that they will be given the ability to use their mouths to speak for God (cf. Exodus 4:16 where Aaron is designated as Moses' "mouthpiece"; Jeremiah 15:19 where Jeremiah is said to be "as God's mouth"). Thus, their words would be God's Word.

give them **words and wisdom.** If there were any way to say more clearly that their preaching would be inspired by the Spirit, I don't know what it is. Their messages, Jesus declared, would be **given** to them by the Holy Spirit, Who would **teach** them exactly what to say (presumably, during the very act of speaking, in ways similar to the way He would inspire them as they wrote Scripture). And because at the time when they needed it such total assistance would be available, they were told not to **worry** (or be concerned) about **what** they would say or **how** they would say it. Moreover, they would find it useless **to practice their defense beforehand** since all they would need in the way of **wisdom** or **words** to confound those who might oppose would be provided by the Spirit on the spot when needed. Those words sketch out a comprehensive program of inspiration.[1]

I suggest then that the first concern of the Holy Spirit which He promised to provide help for is the **what** of preaching. It was of the utmost importance to Him to see that *the right thing* was preached. *Content* was essential. The message could not be garbled, could not be weakened, could not be amended, could not be embellished. It had to be the truth, the whole truth, and nothing but the truth *of God*. As the Spirit brooded over the deep at creation, so too He would brood over the preaching of the apostles in the early days of the church, making it His concern. He would have no other foundation laid than that which was proper.

This concern for content is set forth clearly in at least the first three verses, and by implication in the fourth. Notice the

---

[1] Perhaps I should say a word about the term "inspiration." I am using it here and throughout the book to indicate the divine impartation of all that is needed to preach. While the apostles actually spoke, they were immediately taught what to say at the time when they needed it. The word *inspiration* is so commonly used to refer to inerrancy in the writing of the Scriptures that it may easily be transferred to this action of the Spirit in fully enabling the apostles to preach God's Word without error. The process seems to be similar, if not identical. However, I recognize that the word inspiration, coming as it does from II Timothy 3:16, is a poor translation of the original Greek which

recurring phrase **what you will say**. That is plainly a promise to provide proper content. This content, we are told, would be **given** to the apostles as they spoke. Moreover, we read that the Spirit would **teach** them **what** they **ought to say** (Luke 12:12). There can be no doubt, then, about the first concern of the Holy Spirit in inspiring the preaching of the apostles.

Given this concern of the Spirit, every preacher must also make content a major concern in preaching. If the Spirit went to the trouble of superintending the preaching content of the apostles, He expects you to consider content of great importance. But notice—without question, the content that would be forthcoming would be that which God supplied. It would be His truth. There was no place in what was said for human opinion, speculation, psychological advice or a hundred other things that men regularly introduce into the pulpit. The only way for us today to approximate what the Spirit did is to preach the *Word of God*. And that means nothing but what God has told us in the Bible.

Since that is true, preacher, you may not be slack in your work of exegesis. You must be certain that what you preach is the truth of the Scriptures. You must please the Spirit by your concern for what you preach. Everything isn't fair game for preaching. Those things that the same Spirit inspired the apostles to write in the Scriptures are available to you. From start to finish, the content of the apostolic message is Spirit-inspired. It is our task today, then, to use this carefully designed and executed

---

might more readily be translated *expiration*. Literally, it means "breathed out by God," and refers to the fact that the written words of Scripture are every bit as much God's Word as if He had spoken them by means of breath. But since the word "inspired" is used to refer to the idea of material divinely given by the "moving" of the Spirit in the apostles as they wrote (II Peter 1:21), it conveys the same thought that is present in the verses we are examining. I retain the word "inspiration," therefore, in spite of some strong reservations. For a more detailed exposition of the passage in II Timothy 3:15-17, see my book *How to Help People Change*.

work of the Spirit in our preaching. There is no excuse for doing anything else.

The second factor which the Holy Spirit was concerned with, according to the prediction of Jesus, was **words**: *the right language*. The verses in question uniformly mention **how** the apostles would present the inspired content and assured them that they would be given the **words** by which they would deliver their messages. There would neither be stumbling around seeking the right terminology nor a need to correct what one said. The proper content would be delivered in words that exactly suited it and conveyed precisely what the Spirit wished the listener to hear. Divinely-inspired content would in no way be lessened in its impact by purely human efforts to express it. As the apostles used their own vocabularies and other language traits to write the Scriptures under the moving power of the Spirit, so too they expressed the message out of the language they had acquired. How, then, could what they spoke be said to be linguistically inspired? There is no problem here. The sovereign God Who orders and controls all things, in His providential dealings with these apostles, so arranged their backgrounds, the circumstances in which they wrote and spoke, and the development of their several ways of writing and speaking that He could produce from their various styles His truth in the very language that He deemed best for presenting it. And, in the process, He in no way violated their personalities or responsible action. They were not robots. This seems very difficult for us to comprehend, perhaps, because we are not omnipotent, omnipresent and omniscient. But He is; and that makes all the difference. We don't have to understand it; we simply need to believe it.

So it is not at all a matter of indifference how one addresses a congregation in the Name of Christ. Clearly, it was a concern of the Spirit that *the right thing* be delivered in *the right words*. Survey the speeches of the apostles recorded in the book of Acts, and you will learn something about what sort of language they used. Obviously, it was not some peculiar language that no one else ever spoke. It was the language of the people to whom they spoke. It was neither stilted nor profane, but it was the *koine* (the common language of everyday business and social activity) that the Spirit inspired, heightened of course by the subject matter. One of the reasons given for maintaining the King James Version—with all of its problems—is the "majestic language" in which it is written. Sorry to inform you, the original writings could hardly be called "majestic."

I can never forget taking a course in *koine* Greek at Johns Hopkins University, where I majored in that language. It was my first class with the head of the Classics Department, who was a *koine* expert. I was the only student in class.

He said, "I see that you are headed for the ministry. I confess that even though I have spent many years reading inscriptions, papyri, and the like from the period, I have never translated the New Testament. Let's translate the New Testament this semester."

In disbelief, I said, "The whole New Testament?"

"Sure, why not?" was his reply.

"Well, do you have any idea how long it is?" I inquired.

"I guess it is pretty long," he conceded. "We'll just translate Paul, then."

"All of Paul?" I asked.

"All of Paul," he replied.

So, the next week we began with Romans 1. He called on me to translate the chapter. Being the only student, there was no question about who would be called to do so. I did so. At the conclusion, he sat there silently shaking his head. I was sure that I had made some egregious errors and that my first performance with the head of the department was getting off to a very poor start. I waited for his comments. Finally, this is what I heard. "Why, that is language I wouldn't have expected to find in the New Testament. Here, look at this word. Paul is using gutter language.

Here, look at this…." And off he went, pointing out word after word and expression after expression that he knew from the common language of the streets. It was like an unconverted Greek of Paul's day reading the New Testament for the first time. He came across Gnostic terms in Colossians, terms the average businessman would understand in other places, etc. Each time he would excitedly point out to me that he knew these words from the everyday inscriptions and papyri with which he was familiar. It was a course I shall never forget! It became crystal clear that the Bible was written for the common man, not for the philosophers or the academic crowd. The preaching of the apostles at every point approximates that which we find in their writings. The choice of vocabulary and style evidently had precisely the same ends in view in both instances.

Moving on, we see that not only did Jesus' promises cover content (the right thing) and language (the right words), but also **wisdom**: *the right manner* in which the message would be proclaimed. While this probably was referred to in the comments about teaching them **how to do so** (Luke 12) and **how you will say it** (Matthew 10) along with the choice of terminology and style, there is no question that manner is referred to in Luke 21, where Jesus promised to provide the wisdom needed to preach effectively. This wisdom would be so powerful that opponents would melt before it. The One Who spoke of becoming wise as serpents and harmless as doves saw to it that the apostles in their preaching would manifest these abilities.

There is, therefore, no excuse for sloppy reasoning or flawed thinking in the proclamation of God's Word. There is no place for the preacher's alienating people by his own deficiencies which call attention to himself instead of the message. The manner of the messenger, then, is of great significance to the Holy Spirit, or Jesus would not have mentioned it in His predictions.

The right thing, presented in the right language and the right manner—one that honors God and facilitates rather than hinders the preaching that one does—are the first three concerns of the inspiring Spirit that are immediately noticeable. What of the fourth?

The fourth factor is that the Spirit would do these things for the apostles *at the right time:* **in that hour, in that very hour**. The divinely-given help would come when it was needed. The apostles could count on it being **"taught"** or **"given"** to them at the appropriate moment. They would not need this help before-hand, but as they endeavored to proclaim the truth (often in very trying situations) they would discover that the exact content, the proper language and the wisest manner in which to present it was always at their disposal. There would be no hemming or hawing. They would have no regrets later that they "might have done better if…." Right off the bat they *did* the best that the Spirit could expect—*each* time.

Now, being imperfect creatures, nothing we ever say in this life will come even close to the inspired preaching of the apostles. They truly were unique. This inspiration of the Spirit made them so. But it certainly ought to be our desire to increasingly become able to say things well *at the outset.* That, of course, is something that the prayerful effort of each preacher of the Word must seek. Paul speaks of **"making"** one's **"progress[1] apparent to all"** (I Timothy 4:15). If there is no evident progress in the preaching of a minister, something is lacking. It must be remedied. We must strive for full fluency.[2]

All of these things that I have been briefly touching on in this chapter will be dealt with in a fuller way as we progress. But for now, let it suffice to say that the Spirit-inspired apostolic preaching clearly evidenced the four issues that have been set forth and thereby set for us an example that ought to have strong influence upon what we consider important in our own preaching of the Scriptures.

---

[1] The word *prokope* ("progress") used here means striking out into new territory.

[2] I shall describe what I mean by this later on.

Chapter 2
The Holy Spirit Did It

Jesus did what He said He would do. The four concerns of the Holy Spirit were worked out in the preaching of the apostles. Let us summarize again what those concerns were:

1. The Right Thing (what): content
2. The Right Words (how): language
3. The Right Manner (how): wisdom
4. The Right Time (when): timeliness

These four concerns might not be exclusive; the Spirit also may have had other concerns. But it is these four that are pointed out in the words of Christ as He described the inspiration that the Holy Spirit would provide. It is therefore these four concerns that we shall focus upon.

The first thing that we must recognize is that, true to His Word, Jesus sent His Spirit. The Spirit's coming had many ramifications. While still on this earth, in a human body that was limited by time and space, Jesus (as the God-man) could be only one place at a time. The Spirit, not bound by any such physical limitations, could be with all members of the church wherever they were in the world. That, of course, included the apostles as they traveled in various directions preaching throughout the *oikoumene* (that is the "civilized" or Roman world to which they carried the gospel, cf. Colossians 1:6, 23). The coming of the Spirit is what made the fulfillment of the promise of inspired preaching possible. Indeed, if we see anything in the book of Acts, it is that the Holy Spirit, Who was dramatically ushered in on the Day of Pentecost, dominated the activity of the apostles as they carried the gospel from Jerusalem to Judea and Samaria and to the uttermost parts of the world. They were "filled with the

Spirit." It is in Acts preeminently that we see the fulfillment of Jesus' promised inspiration.

But before examining how these four elements played out in the preaching itself, let us take up a matter or two about the subject at hand. The predictions found in the Gospels that we have been studying speak about inspiration that would be given in times of persecution or trial. They talk about times when the apostles would be hauled up before governors and kings. They speak about making a **defense** at such times. It is clear that they would be given what they needed to represent Jesus Christ in such circumstances. But was the inspiration that they would receive limited to such occasions, or did it extend to other preaching situations as well?

The latter seems undoubtedly to be true. This I say because in looking at the speech of Peter on the Day of Pentecost— which in no sense approximated a trial before an authority— inspiration was clearly present and operative. On that occasion, when Peter was privileged to use the first of the two keys to unlock the door of the church to the Jews, he spoke under inspiration. Those who were with him seem to have been granted a similar boon:

> And they were all *filled with the Holy Spirit* and began to speak revelatory words in different languages *as the Spirit gave them ability.*
>
> (Acts 2: 4, emphasis added)

The Greek term *apophtheggomai* that I have translated **to speak revelatory words** is a rare one. In the New Testament, it appears only here in verses 4 and 14 and in Acts 26:25. It was used of pagan oracles and seers who purported to speak under divine inspiration. In the Septuagint, it was employed by the translators of the Old Testament to describe inspired prophetic speech (see I Chronicles 25:1; Deuteronomy 32:2; Zechariah 10:2; Ezekiel 13:9). Marvin R. Vincent says that it refers to a "clear, loud utterance under miraculous impulses" (*Word Studies, Vol. I,* p.449). There is no question, then, that on this occasion Peter gave the address that is recorded under divine influence. The word could refer to nothing less. That means that while Jesus promised inspiration in times of trial, He did not intend to limit that inspiration to such occasions. By revealing to them that the Spirit would help them speak in these difficult situations, He was able to encourage the disciples beforehand. But wherever they were spokesmen for the Lord, it is clear that they were granted a fulfillment of the promise. Listen to what J. M. Stifler had to say about Peter's speech in Acts 2.

> Christian eloquence is not a gift of nature but of grace. Piety is necessary to the best oratory. But when Peter's address on this morning is studied, we have still more convincing proof of the Spirit's presence. In its adroitness, in the arrangement of the arguments, in its analysis, in its steering clear of Jewish prejudices, in its appeal and effect, it is without a peer among the products of uninspired men. As an example of persuasive argument it has no rival. The more it is studied the more its beauty and power are disclosed. And yet it is the work of a Galilean fisherman, without culture or training, and his maiden effort.... Who taught the provincial fisherman this bright piece of oratorical wisdom?... Who taught the unschooled Peter this perfection in argumentation? It implies a metaphysician's knowledge of the hearer's reason and feeling. He knows just how the auditor must be addressed to be won. Beethoven could not play on the pianoforte with more mastery than Peter shows in touching the many keys in the human heart.

Again, how did Peter miss the pitfall of the novice in not making in this address a great deal of his own personal experience?... Peter had seen and heard and handled Jesus after the resurrection. He was, besides, an appointed witness. And yet he makes the very least of this office. There is but a single mention, at the close of the second argument, in the words, "whereof we are all witnesses" (v. 32)....
Who taught Peter to make this limited use of his own personal knowledge of the resurrection? And who taught him the higher wisdom to put this particular argument in just the right place?

Pages might be written on the grandeur of this address, which, it must not be forgotten, was extemporaneous. But this is sufficient to show that he who wrote it was either under supernatural influence, or was a supernatural person. To deny the inspiration of the address is to cast us on the other horn of the dilemma, that Peter was more than a mortal man. It does not relieve the question much to say that Luke or anyone else put it in Peter's mouth. For then Luke, or that other supposititious person, must be more than mortal. The structure of the speech transcends human power. It must have come from God's Spirit.[1]

Allowing for possible overstatement here and there in Stifler's exposition of the sermon, nevertheless there seems to be no doubt that he has successfully raised the important issues when considering Peter's Pentecostal address. There is no way—short

---

[1] J.M. Stifler. *An Introduction to the Study of the Book of Acts.* Revell: New York (1892), pp.18-22. This book is one of the seminal studies in the book of Acts, a volume that every preacher ought to seek to obtain even though it is currently out of print.

of divine inspiration—that Peter could have given that address. The Spirit Who filled others to speak in revelatory tongues and prophetic words, in addition moved Peter to address the crowd. Here, then, is the first striking instance of the fulfillment of the inspiration promise of the Lord Jesus Christ.[1] Thus, as Stifler and Timothy Dwight aver, the apostles experienced the inspiring power of the Spirit in proclaiming the Word from the outset of their ministries.[2] No sooner had the Spirit descended than He began to exercise His inspiring function. And we see that it was not only in times of danger and persecution, but also on other occasions that He inspired apostolic preaching.[3]

We come now to a closer look at the four concerns of the Spirit. First, there is The Right Thing—the **what**: content. The message that the apostles preached had to be consistent, it had to be untainted by human additions or subtractions; it had to be the pure Word of God. Inspiration assured that. As you go through the book of Acts, one thing is impressive: the gospel (the primary message of the apostles in their evangelistic preaching) was clearly articulated. Whenever Luke brings the reader close enough to hear what is proclaimed in one of the several speeches

---

[1] Stifler is not alone in his understanding of the divine inspiration of apostolic preaching. Timothy Dwight put it succinctly when he wrote, "each inspired man was, as to his preaching, or his writing, absolutely preserved from error." *Theology Explained and Defended in a Series of Sermons,* Vol. 2, Harper and Brothers: New York (1854), p. 137. See also Hendriksen, *Mark,* p. 521.

[2] It is instructive to note that, for the most part, it is in older rather than in more recent works that one finds a recognition of the inspiration of apostolic preaching. It is time to revive this all but forgotten truth.

[3] Luke usually explains something on its first occasion, then expects the reader to assume that to apply to other such occasions thereafter without having to reiterate the fact. This is true, for instance, about the abbreviation of the discourses that he records (Acts 2:40). One may presume that it is true also of the inspiration of apostolic preaching that he describes under the rare, rich and suggestive term *apophtheggomai.*

that he records, he shows how the two points of the gospel (enumerated by Paul in I Corinthians 15:1-4) were taught. These two points are the death of Jesus Christ for[1] sinners and His bodily resurrection from the dead. Over and over, that message, adapted to each audience, is set forth plainly and with absolute certainty as the heart and core of the Christian faith.[2] This consistency, doubtless, is due to the work of the Spirit of God. The clearly Christological understanding of the Old Testament Scriptures that is evidenced by Peter and Stephen,[3] for instance, was the result of the Spirit's inspiration.

Jesus made other promises which probably refer principally to the apostles' ability to write inerrantly. They are found in the Gospel of John:

> The Holy Spirit...will teach you everything and remind you of everything that I told you.
>
> (John 14:26)

> But when the Spirit of truth comes, He will guide you into all truth... and He will tell you things to come.
>
> (John 16:13)

In these verses there is a plain and unmistakable claim for inspiration. The Gospel writers would be reminded of all that they had seen and heard so as to write accurate accounts of Jesus' ministry. The Spirit would guide them around faulty and erroneous interpretations of events, teaching them instead the meaning and intentions of the other biblical writers. Moreover, He would reveal to them events that would occur in the future. In other words, they would have the unerring help of the Spirit of God in

---

[1] The Greek word is *huper*, "on behalf of."
[2] Cf. 2:23, 24; 3:13, 15; 4:10; 5:29-32; 10:39-41; 13:28-33; 23:6; 26:23, where the resurrection only is mentioned. Obviously, Luke presupposes a prior death.
[3] Inspiration on special occasions (at least) seems to have been extended to others beyond the twelve (cf. Acts 7:55).

all that had to do with the message about which they wrote and spoke.

While the verses (especially the first) may have primarily to do with the writing of the New Testament Scriptures, what was taught by the Spirit for that purpose could not help but affect what the apostles spoke. The two things were bound up together in each individual preacher. After all, individuals are whole persons who cannot divorce one aspect of their lives from the rest. So, in addition to what we have already seen in the verses that directly pertain to preaching, we see here unmistakable proof that the content that the apostles received was divinely inspired.

In the second concern we recognize the Spirit's interest in language. Ever since the evil one attacked God's Word in the Garden of Eden there has been a struggle with maintaining truthful language. Satan substituted words for the true Word of God, words that were calculated to lead man astray. God had said that Adam and Eve might eat freely of every tree of the garden, but that they must not eat of the tree of the knowledge of good and evil. Satan's words, however, implied that God had forbidden them to eat of *all* the trees. God's grace and generosity were thereby impugned and Eve was cast into the role of a defender and clarifier of what God had said. In her reply, she not only corrected Satan, but then added a twist of her own, saying that God had forbidden them even to *touch* the tree in the midst of the garden. Already, at this pristine stage of human history, the problem of language had arisen. The meaning of what God had said and the proper communication of truth became a prime matter of concern. The distortion of God's truth has continued to be a serious problem ever since, down through human history. The issue is so important because it is by His Word that man maintains a proper relationship to God.

No wonder, then, that God did not depend upon unaided and fallible sinful man to remember or correctly reproduce the truths concerning His Son and His atoning death on the cross. Truth—

including the language by which it would be conveyed (that is to say, the very *words and expressions* used in doing so)—had to be shored up by the process of inspiration. So God presented His saving Word about the cross to fallen mankind in human language by means of divine assistance that rendered what was preached and written inerrant.

The apostle Paul, who also received this endowment from the Spirit (I Corinthians 7:40), had this to say about the matter: **I didn't deliver my message or preach in persuasive words of man's wisdom, but with proof and power provided by the Spirit** (I Corinthians 2:4). The words that he preached were not manipulative like those of the Sophists of his day. They were words given by God's Spirit and used powerfully by Him to persuade people properly. And Paul went on to say, the **things about which we speak** were not communicated **in words taught by human wisdom but in those that are taught by the Spirit** (I Corinthians 2:13). His explanation seems to mirror the prophetic words of Jesus from John's Gospel quoted earlier. The expression **taught by the Spirit** could be a direct reference. At any rate, Paul said that the very words that he used were not those that he had learned to use in the schools of Tarsus or Jerusalem, but they were the words the Spirit taught him to use in preaching. So, the Spirit extended His gift of inspiration beyond content to language as well.

The third thing that Jesus said the Spirit would concern Himself with was the manner of the presentation. Good words and proper language may be destroyed by a flawed approach to listeners. The message had to be adapted to all sorts and conditions of men (to use the handy expression from the prayer book). If Luke intended to do anything in the book of Acts it was to show that the gospel message was adaptable to every sort of person from every sort of background. Under the Spirit's guidance, Luke selected various messages that were preached to all manner of persons. The first apparent distinction to note is between

Jews and Gentiles. Sermons by Peter, Stephen and Paul reproduced in the early part of Acts were delivered to Jewish audiences. Even a casual perusal of these sermons shows a very heavy reliance upon the Scriptures. In addition, there is a recital of the history of God's dealings with Israel up to the death and resurrection of Christ together with an infallible interpretation of this. That, of course, is an example of their properly adapting to a Jewish congregation for whom the Bible was considered an authority.

But one can discern a radical change of approach as the message went out to the Gentiles: the Bible was not quoted at all. Was the apostle Paul accommodating the message, paring it down for the sake of acceptance? Of course not! Indeed, had he attempted to do so, the Spirit would not have allowed it. No, the very same message was preached, but the Old Testament was not used overtly because it did not hold any authority for those outside the people of Israel. That was simply the evidence of wisdom. It is clear that, as Jesus predicted, the Spirit *did* extend his superintendence of apostolic preaching to the gift of **wisdom** (Luke 21). Once more, consider Paul's explanation in I Corinthians as he discussed his preaching: **we speak, not in words taught by human wisdom but in those that are taught by the Spirit**. The contrast in the verse is between words of man's "wisdom" and those taught to him by the Spirit. By these words, he positioned himself in a sphere outside of that which can be learned by human wisdom alone; his claim is that he relied on the wisdom of the Spirit as he preached.

This spiritual wisdom taught Paul to **combine spiritual teaching with spiritual words** (v. 2:13^b). Spiritual words equal the words that the Spirit gave him—words that, in contrast to all others, came from the Spirit. This important fact, that has bearing not only on the manner in which one approaches his listeners but also on the sort of language with which he does so, shows how inspiration was of a piece. You could not remove any one of the four concerns and still retain the other three. Words given in the wisdom of the Spirit are those with which preachers today ought to concern themselves. But we shall have more to say about this later.[1]

Finally, the fourth concern is timeliness: **in that very hour**. The Spirit was concerned that the apostles not be at a loss for words—His words. So as occasion arose, He provided (in a manner beyond our ability to understand) exactly what the preacher needed by way of content, language and wisdom in knowing how to approach a given audience. How handy that would be for many of us today who from time to time (or more often) find ourselves searching for these very things. To be able to size up a situation, know what a given congregation needs at any given time, and be able to couch the message in clear, persuasive and appropriate terms is the desire of all true preachers. That is what the Spirit provided.

Timeliness and appropriateness, along with the ability to fashion sentences that express these thoughts in the best way, is what the Spirit taught these early preachers. Therefore, I will also address how we may satisfy these concerns in order to please rather than grieve the Spirit as we preach. But right here we must simply understand these concerns of His. In Athens, before the council of the Areopagus (Acts 17), we see Paul putting together a remarkable array of ideas, allusions and truths in order to bring home the message of the death and resurrection of Christ. The acuteness with which he baffled both the Stoics and Epicureans—by turning their own stupidity in erecting an altar to an unknown god against them and to his own advantage—shows Paul's reliance upon the Spirit's great wisdom.[2] This wis-

---

[1] Other matters demonstrate the adaptive wisdom of the Spirit. For instance, Luke reproduced sample messages to a rustic in Lystra and to the sophisticated audience in Athens, showing how the same message could be adapted to each.

[2] Paul was given a preliminary hearing. People were accusing him of setting

dom was granted in the moment of delivery, along with the various elements woven into this sermon that skillfully refute the principal beliefs of the two philosophies represented in the audience, while at the same time proclaiming the truth. An obvious need that all of us would-be later day preachers share is the ability to do as the Spirit enabled Paul to do on that occasion. Again, we shall later discuss how we may begin to acquire this readiness.

For now it is enough for us to say that we understand more thoroughly what the Spirit desires to find in our preaching. The big question is how to attain to such high standards.

---

forth new gods, one of the two charges on which Socrates had been convicted and executed by this very body. Here, deflecting any such possibility in his case, Paul told them that he would introduce them to the God Whom they did not know and sought to worship in ignorance. This was one of the greatest adaptations to a possibly hostile audience in the history of preaching.

Chapter 3

The Spirit's First Concern

As we saw, *content* is one main concern of the Holy Spirit. His inspiration was given to assure accuracy in content, a doctrine that we refer to as inerrancy. But there is more to His concern about accuracy. We discovered that the emphasis on truth had to do with revelation as well (John 16:13). New material would be brought to light by the apostles. This prophecy of Jesus, that the Spirit would guide into **all truth**, was clearly fulfilled. Listen to the apostle Paul:

> ...by revelation the secret was made known to me, even as I wrote you briefly before...which was not made known to human beings in other generations as it now has been revealed to His holy apostles and prophets by the Spirit. (Ephesians 3:3, 5)

The apostles and prophets[1] were given both a more thorough understanding of the Old Testament than had **been made known before** and brand new revelation necessary for the New Covenant churches to know. They recorded revelatory information in the Scriptures, but also preached it wherever they went. Not all of the apostles left us inspired writings, but the promise of inspiration in preaching was to all of the apostles. In a sense, then, we should look upon inspired preaching as primary and the recording of it (under inspiration as well) as secondary.

Take a look at their claim to inspiration. Paul could write: **What I am writing...is God's commandment** (I Corinthians 14:37). Paul's writing is acknowledged by all Bible-believing

---

[1] "Prophets" most likely refers to New Testament writers other than the apostles.

Christians to be God's truth; but that the content of his preaching was also revelatory (and therefore God's inerrant commandments) is not so widely acknowledged. But Paul had no difficulty in saying, **To us**[1] **God revealed it by His Spirit** (I Corinthians 2:10). From the context of I Corinthians 2 it is clear that he was here speaking about his *preaching* (see vv. 4, 6, 7, 13). The word "revelation" always refers to data that come directly from God. It is not human speculation or discovery. It is *divinely*-given information, truth that He inerrantly provided for His people through those He had chosen to make it known. Jesus predicted that truth would be given, and Paul tells us in unmistakable terms that the prediction had come true.

We must understand, then, how important the matter of content is to the Spirit (Who, notice, is frequently mentioned in the verses telling of the fulfillment of the promise of inspiration as well as in the verses in which the promise was made). The truth that was revealed was varied. One aspect of it (at least; if not all) is referred to as the **deposit**. In his last letter, in which he is handing over his ministry to his younger associate Timothy, Paul speaks of having entrusted truth to him in a **pattern of healthy words** that he expected Timothy to **guard** (II Timothy 1:12-14). The familiar hymn based on verse 12 has it backwards. Both the one who hands over a sum of money to a teller at the window of a bank and the teller may each refer to that which shifts hands as "my deposit." That is, literally, what Paul is talking about in these verses. The song writer takes the view that it was Paul entrusting his life into God's hands. But the opposite is actually the case. Paul was talking about the revelatory deposit that God gave him, his faithful preservation of it, and his handing over of it to Timothy. It is this that he referred to in verse 14 when exhorting Timothy to **guard the good deposit which has been entrusted to you**. Paul was about to die; he was handing the

---

[1] Paul included himself in the promises made to the apostolic band.

torch to Timothy. This torch was the **good deposit**.[1]

Timothy was to preserve the truth that God had deposited with Paul and which Paul was now passing on to him; and when the time came for Timothy to die, he too was to do the same: **the things that you heard from me before many witnesses pass along to trustworthy persons who will be competent to teach others also** (II Timothy 2:2). It should be evident from these words that there was important content that was revealed, preached and passed on. What Paul was concerned about was that this wonderful revelation he had received would continue to be taught in the church. Unfortunately, in time, some dropped the torch of inspiration since the fullness of the deposit was soon lost to the world.

Revelation that was recorded by the Old Testament prophets was primarily verbal. Again and again the prophet was called upon to preach to the people of Israel as a part of the revelatory "burden" he received from the Lord. Later, that spoken revelation (or, at least a summary of it) was written down. Doubtless, that is why one of the favorite terms used to identify the prophetic Scriptures is the *Word* **of God**. There is no reason to suspect that the process was different in the case of the New Testament apostles. What was first spoken was later written. That is plainly true of the sermons and the speeches recorded in the book of Acts. Some of the general epistles, such as James, appear to be a compilation of sermon materials that had been preached many times before. And, for instance, when you look at the similarity of the material in Colossians and Ephesians, you are almost required to believe that much of the material was what Paul regularly preached.[2]

---

[1] Notice also I Timothy 6: 20: **Timothy, guard that which was entrusted to you**. The danger was that false teachers had entered the church who wanted to substitute their message for the deposit of revelatory truth that Paul was handing down.

[2] Preachers like to preach from Paul and Peter. That is because much of what

In I Corinthians 15:1-4 Paul speaks of having **announced. . . the message of good news** which he says was **of** the **greatest importance**, and which he assures them **he received** and **delivered** to them. What he **received**, was received by means of divine revelation; what he **delivered**, similarly, was delivered by means of revelatory preaching. Listen further to how Paul describes the source of his preaching:

> I want you to know, brothers, that the good news that was announced by me isn't according to human ideas, because I didn't receive it from a human being, nor was I taught it, but I received it as a revelation from Jesus Christ.   (Galatians 1:11, 12)

Plainly, these verses delineate the process by which the truth of God was conveyed to His church. Divine revelation, deposited first with the apostles, was then given through preaching. From all of these sources (the list could be enlarged) we may confidently say that the message Paul (and the other apostles) preached was *divinely* given. So, once more, we see that the Spirit is concerned about content.

What was this content like? From the above quotations it is evident that the gospel message was a part of the content. But that is not all. The same verses that speak of the good news reveal, for instance, that the place of the Gentiles (as part of the New Testament church) was also taught. It seems, then, that it was not simply *some* matters (for instance, those of the **greatest importance**) that were revealed, but also all the details that were necessary for the welfare of the church.

This fact should take no one by surprise. After all, during the forty days between the resurrection and the ascension when Jesus spoke to the disciples **about matters pertaining to God's**

---

is included in their letters is written in preaching form. It must be remembered that they were preachers who happened to be writing through an amanuensis. Thus a good bit of that material is very much like preaching.

empire (Acts 1:3), He probably could not cover everything necessary for them to know. And even if He had done so the disciples would probably not have remembered all things as they should. Remember, the Spirit was sent to *remind* them **of everything that** Jesus **told** them (John 14:26). Those matters which the Spirit would bring to their remembrance doubtless included Jesus' teaching during the forty day period, as well as His teaching before the cross. And—keep in mind—Paul was not included among those who were instructed during the forty day interval. *Inspired revelation* of that information—which extended to his preaching and writing—therefore, also was essential.

But *doctrinal* revelatory content, as important as it was, was not the only province of the Spirit's inspiration. Applicatory materials, that were very much a part of the content of New Testament preaching, were equally superintended by the Spirit. When Paul wrote about husbands and wives and about marriage and divorce in response to those who doubted, he assured them (with a bit of irony), **I also think that I have God's Spirit** (I Corinthians 7:40). That is to say, what he taught about such matters was revelatory. The apostle reminded the Thessalonians, **when we were with you, as you know, we told you beforehand that you were going to be afflicted, just as indeed it has happened** (I Thessalonians 3:4). Clearly, the ability to know something of the future and impart that information to the churches in one's preaching (a Spirit-given capacity that Jesus also promised in John 16:13) was a part of the applicatory function of inspired preaching. Here, as in I Corinthians 7:26, 29 where he predicted a **coming crisis**, assured the Corinthian church that **the time** [was] **short**, and advised them how to live through the coming persecution, we see prophetic inspiration at work once more (see also II Thessalonians 3:10).

So, it seems that the Spirit was revealing truth not merely abstractly but also in applicatory form, in response to situations in which the apostles found themselves as they preached and counseled the churches. The content with which He was concerned, therefore, was also truth *applied*. The Christian minister today may learn from biblical examples what to preach in terms of raw doctrine, but also about how that doctrine affects life.

Here is where much modern day orthodox preaching goes astray. Preachers throw out solid, meaty doctrine in their messages to congregations, but rarely tell them how that doctrine should affect life. But all doctrine is designed to deal with life. It is an egregious error to bifurcate the two. Paul highlighted this connection between doctrine and life in the opening words of his letter to Titus when he wrote that God had made him His **slave and apostle...to promote the faith of God's chosen people and the full knowledge of the *truth that is in the interest of godliness*** (Titus 1:1). Truth is not to be learned for the sake of truth itself. It is not to be learned to pack one's head full of the right answers for use during the next Sunday School Bible quiz. **Truth** is intended to produce **godliness** (that is, lives that reflect the moral attributes of God). While truth is essential to godliness—there is no godliness apart from the truth of God—godliness is the essential fruit[1] of that truth when it is at work in one's life. The two are as solidly wedded in the Scriptures as are faith and works.

The apostles' task included more than preaching the **full knowledge** of the truth to which Paul referred, even though through this knowledge the Spirit at work in them was building the church of which Jesus spoke in Matthew 16:18 and following. Note that Paul explicitly said that the kingdom that they were constructing by means of preaching and writing consisted of **righteousness and peace and joy by the Holy Spirit** (Romans 14:17). As Paul observed, the sanctifying Spirit was active in the work. In addition to the preaching of the gospel, the

---

[1] The fruit of the Spirit (Galatians 5) is the result of the Spirit's application of His revealed truth to individual believers.

Spirit used the applicatory preaching and teaching of which we have been speaking to bring this about.

So when we speak of content, we are talking about more than truth imparted; the Spirit was concerned also about truth implemented. We are saying that the Spirit was busy assisting the apostles as they founded and built up the church in its most holy faith (cf. Jude 20). While there is a human dimension involved in edification, as Jude notes when mentioning prayer, there was also a divine element that had to do with the Spirit: **praying** was to be *by the Holy Spirit*. Paul tells us in Romans 8 that the Spirit helps us even in those prayers. So, it is not unreasonable to think of His inspiring content relating to the *practical* application of truth that He would use in bringing about righteousness, peace and joy. This sanctifying content was proclaimed by the apostles through preaching and writing.

Indeed, the **helpful Word**[1] **of God** that Paul had preached to the Ephesians, he told their elders when departing from them, would be **able to build** them **up** (Acts 20:32). What was this Word like? Paul reminded the elders that he had *proclaimed* **God's whole counsel** (vv. 27) and that he had **held back** (literally, furled and stowed away) nothing that might be **beneficial** to them when preaching (**declaring**) God's Word to them (vv. 20, 27). So, what the Spirit enabled Paul to preach had to do with *all* that God had revealed (His whole counsel; i.e., the counsel revealed to Paul and the apostles by Him), and it was declared to be **beneficial** and **helpful**[2] (vv. 20, 32). The whole counsel of God includes all the content that would help one to love God and love his neighbor. John makes this point when he writes, **This is the message that you heard from the beginning, that we should love one another** (I John 3:11). Evidently, the inspired preaching in the church that was designed to build believers up,

---

[1] Literally, "Word of His grace." Grace, here, has to do with the assistance (help) God provides for His own.
[2] Not merely instructive.

early on (**from the beginning**) had a practical bent. It was not mere instruction; there was a hortatory element as well. And should there be any doubt about the fact, John declared that love for one's brother was a **commandment that we have from Him** (I John 4:21). It was a divinely-inspired, revelatory commandment. The indicative and the imperative are found side-by-side in inspired preaching. That means that the content that the Holy Spirit was concerned to reveal was full-bodied; this "whole counsel" involved more than doctrine. In fact, it would seem that *everything* that the apostles preached—whether indicative or imperative—is included in that phrase.

Now, we have seen the nature of the Spirit's first concern. The **what** (the right thing) involved all that they preached. It is not as though certain facts were revealed and then the apostles were to improvise on those facts out of their personal resources. As we shall see when we come to discuss the other three concerns, the Spirit effected far more. His inspiration went beyond full content.

But the question now arises, how can we benefit from the knowledge that we have so far acquired? So what if the apostles were inspired as to the content that they preached? After all, we have no such inspiration. The value of knowing about the Spirit's work in the apostles is that preachers today can learn from them by emulating their preaching. As they study the preaching reflected in the epistles and recorded in Acts, they can be assured that they are reading the sort of content of which the Holy Spirit approves. They may learn what truths were presented and what sort of applicatory content the apostles made use of. Therefore, the study of preaching in the New Testament—for its content— is of great assistance (one might even say is absolutely necessary) if he would seek to please His Lord by his content in preaching.

This book is not a study of the *specific* content of apostolic preaching (though, here and there, I have intimated something along those lines). My intention has been merely to draw the broad outlines that I hope many will consider of the highest priority to pursue in their study of preaching. No one can study for another. Sure, he can report the results of his study; and that can be of limited value. But what makes the greatest impact is the disciplined study that one does for himself. To delve into the New Testament on one's own to see what the apostles said about content, and to look at the specimens preserved by Luke in the Acts of the Apostles, is the way to derive maximum benefit from this book. Preachers who seek to preach as the Spirit wishes them to, ought to spend much time reading and rereading the sermons in Acts.

Each preacher knows his own deficiencies (or ought to). As he studies, therefore, he can focus on what may best improve *his* preaching. My hope is to enlarge the thinking of those who previously have thought of content too narrowly, that those who have considered the mere setting forth of doctrine sufficient will see the error of that view. I hope also, on the other hand, that those whose messages are superficial (because they are almost entirely cast in the imperative mood) will begin to stress the indicative as well. In short, it is my hope that men everywhere will learn to **declare the whole counsel of God**.

There is one more important element in our consideration of content. The content of one's preaching ought to be content found in the Scriptures or that to which the Scriptures point, content that every preacher ought to find sufficient for carrying on his ministry (cf. II Timothy 3:17). Listen to what Paul said to Titus, to whom (evidently) this divine inspiration in preaching had not been granted. After laying out a great deal of information concerning order and discipline in the church, Paul wrote, **Speak these things; urge and convict, with recognition that you have full authority to give orders** (Titus 2:15). That exhortation tells us much about how Paul (the Spirit's inspiring him to write, of course) expected other uninspired preachers to use the words that he and the other apostles penned under inspiration. They were to **preach the Word** (II Timothy 4:2). This Paul **solemnly** called on Timothy to do (v. 1). There should be no question, then, about how the inspired apostles exhorted their uninspired followers to preach (cf. Titus 2:2ff.; 3:8). When the faithful ministries of former preachers (perhaps even apostles are referred to here) are set forth as examples for those to whom the book of Hebrews was written, the writer mentions that they **spoke God's message** (Hebrews 13:7). That was the inspired, apostolic message first preached to and then written down for the church of all ages (cf. also I Peter 4:11). The recurring exhortation that is found in the letters to the seven churches, **Whoever has an ear, let him hear what the Spirit says to the churches**, just about sums up the biblical concern in inspired writing and preaching. In other words, all inspired truth is on the very same level and ought to be heard and obeyed because it is *what* the *Spirit* is saying to His church.

In the light of what the Holy Spirit did in fulfillment of Christ's promise, one can say only that it is absolutely essential for every theological seminary to spend time studying the sermons in the Bible to discover what content the Holy Spirit Who inspired them wishes them to preach. How is it that things are otherwise?

Chapter 4
How to Attain to This

It would be impossible to develop a complete program for attaining the same results as the Holy Spirit set forth as goals—without inspiration. It is impossible for a sinful, limited mind to comprehend all that a perfect, infinite mind could; this difference calls for the preacher to spend the rest of his life attempting to approximate as fully as possible what the Spirit did for the apostles instantaneously. Because the scope of this book is more limited, my real interest is in suggesting some possible routes for him to explore and some ways and means of doing so.

The Holy Spirit helped the apostles preach by providing truth both remembered and newly revealed. And in both cases, what He provided was correct, accurate, and inerrant. Moreover, He helped the apostles preach these truths in ways that greatly impacted the lives of those to whom they preached. He therefore took interest not only in content but also in its application to individual situations. Thus, the sermons in the book of Acts are not *lectures*, delivered from place to place in identical form, but individually honed *sermons* in which truth is applied. Because this truth is applied, it is clear that it was adapted to the various sorts of audiences to which it was delivered. If nothing else, these general principles should stand out clearly. The preacher who wishes to improve his preaching so as to please the Spirit will also provide for his congregation content of the sort just described.

But what course should an uninspired preacher take in order to approximate more and more what the Spirit did for the apostles? First, he should set up a program for himself in which he personally analyzes the sermons in the book of Acts and the comments of the apostles in their letters about how inspiration affected what they did. I have already mentioned some places where these comments were made. There are more, of course.

But take the sermons in Acts. It is my opinion that, knowing that they are Spirit-inspired, if one obtains all the commentaries possible and all the special study materials about the sermons, and works hard on exegeting them, he will in time be in a position to do a sermonic analysis of the content. *What*, precisely, did the Holy Spirit do so as to turn the early preachers into men who "turned the world upside down?" What sort of things did they preach? What did they omit? In what ways was their preaching adapted to the time and circumstance in which it was delivered? What were the results? How were the results tied to the content delivered? Questions like this ought to be asked— and answered.

In order to analyze the content in relationship to other factors and elements in the sermons I suggest that the following grid (which will be helpful for other aspects of sermon analysis that we have not yet considered) may be of use here: COLD SOAP. The mnemonic help that the two words "Cold Soap" provide will enable you to intersect various *elements* of preaching (repre- sented by the word COLD) with the several *factors* of the preaching situation (represented by the word SOAP). By relating those elements to those factors, you will find it possible to deter- mine something about how each affects the others.

	S	O	A	P
C				
O				
L				
D				

The letters COLD stand for	The letters SOAP stand for
CONTENT	SPEAKER
ORGANIZATION	OCCASION
LANGUAGE	AUDIENCE
DELIVERY	PURPOSE

Do you see how the grid is helpful? Let's take an example or two. We have mentioned the fact that the apostles (influenced by the Spirit) preached to Jews and Gentiles, to rustic audiences (at Lystra) and sophisticated ones (at Athens). We also maintained that the *same* message—Jesus' death and resurrection—was declared in all places. But the *other* content (as well as other factors) differed. The same message was adaptable to all. How did the variables affect content?

Relate C and A (Content and Audience). What do you get? The content was adapted to the audience. In preaching to Jews, the content was tightly entwined with Old Testament Scripture quotations. In preaching to Gentiles it was not. In Lystra, where people depended on rainfall as their water source for growing food, Paul spoke of the God of Creation (Acts 14:15) and His benevolence to them in sending them fruitful seasons (v. 17). This was but an introduction to the message of good news into which these words led (v. 21). In Athens, Paul quoted poets they respected to enforce what he said[1] (Acts 17:28). Do you get the idea? If so, why not try using another factor over against the element COLD? Try, for instance, Speaker (the first factor in the word SOAP) in analyzing Peter's sermon on Pentecost. Or, for that matter, how about CONTENT and PURPOSE in the same sermon?

Don't spend too much time at this point with the grid. I am only introducing you to it here in a limited way. When we have

---

[1] Placing an entirely different interpretation upon the poets' words.

worked our way through the other three concerns of the Holy Spirit, you will find it even more useful.[1]

What else is required of a preacher in order to assure good content? Having a solid *hermeneutical* understanding is important. It is from the faithful use of proper principles of interpretation that the correct knowledge of biblical content is derived. The preacher today, unlike the inspired apostle, will not receive revelatory truth. He must depend wholly upon the Bible for a knowledge of the teaching he imparts when preaching. He can find correct doctrine nowhere else.

I suggest that if he has never had a satisfying course in hermeneutics, he ought to take one if possible. If that is not possible, he should buy at least five or six books on the subject and devour them. In my book *What to do on Thursday* I have suggested some things about hermeneutics that may afford a beginning.

It is important for every preacher to be familiar with Hebrew and Greek, the two languages in which the Old and the New Testaments were written. If, for some reason, a choice must be made between which to learn first or which of the two alone must be learned, the decision should be made in favor of Greek. After all, we live in New Testament times and must preach the Old Testament through the insights of the New. Ideally, one should have a working knowledge of both languages, enabling him to get behind the translations to evaluate their renderings of any given passage. Realistically, with all a minister finds himself doing, it is usually impossible for him to keep his languages up to snuff. Most men, having had several courses in Greek and Hebrew, find that they cannot maintain the sort of knowledge of them that enables them to pick up the text and read it without any helps. Of what value, then, is the study of the languages? Supremely, this:

---

[1] In this book, I have advised using only the COLD SOAP grid. It is possible also to use a COLD COLD and also a SOAP SOAP grid as well. The COLD SOAP grid, however, is basic and, I think you will find, the most useful one.

they will be able to understand and use the better commentaries and helps. The language courses will make it possible to follow the reasoning of their authors. That ability is invaluable.

The use of a good theological library is also critical. If a man is concerned to understand the Word as sharply as the good carpenter or stone mason makes an accurate cut (II Timothy 2:15), he will want to have thoroughly understood every passage from all points of view before preaching on it.[1] He will long to become a skillful workman in the Word. If his goal is any less than that, he ought to rethink it.[2] In order to do the very best job of understanding content he will find it necessary to consult the best resources. If he does not have access to a good theological library, there are not only books available, but also all sorts of helps on computer disks at very reasonable prices. There is little excuse for a preacher not to be able to access the helps needed today.

So, a firm acquaintance with the biblical languages, a complete understanding of the principles of hermeneutics, a method for analyzing sermons (the homiletical grid), and access to the best resources available is essential. These four things will go a long way toward helping a preacher preach *the right thing*. However, there is just one more point to be made. All of this is of value only to the one who works hard. Presumably, something of Paul's own human agency was involved (I am not quite sure how) even in the use of the inspired materials imparted to him (cf. Ephesians 6:19, 20; Colossians 4:3, 4).

---

[1] I am not writing to men who buy sermon outlines or who crib their sermons from Spurgeon or others. Such reprehensible actions on the part of a "preacher" mean that he should either repent of these practices or leave the ministry.

[2] For more details, see my book *Committed to Craftsmanship in Biblical Counseling*. What is said there about counseling applies to preaching as well.

Chapter 5

The Spirit's Second Concern

The Holy Spirit is concerned about content, but that content can be enhanced or ruined by the language in which it is proclaimed. His second concern, therefore, is for *the right language*. Words, grammar and style are included in this concern. The phrases **how you will say it** (Matthew 10), **how to do so** (Luke 12), **words[1] and wisdom** (Luke 21) all point to language capabilities (and perhaps, in addition, to manner). Also, consider these words: **you must say what will be given to you** (Matthew 10), and **say whatever is given to you** (Mark 13:11); **the Spirit will teach you... what you ought to say** (Luke 12). Moreover, we read that it will be **the Spirit of My Father speaking in you** (Matthew 10); that **it won't be you speaking, but the Holy Spirit** (Mark 13). These promises all indicate that not only the *what* but also the *how* would be determined by the Spirit. Thus the promise of inspiration included language.

Was the promise fulfilled? Listen to the apostle Paul:

> It is these things about which we speak, not in words taught by human wisdom but in those that are taught by the Spirit, combining spiritual teaching with spiritual words. (I Corinthians 2:13)

His comment couldn't be clearer. The fact is that even the words that he used were from the Spirit. The **spiritual teaching**

---

[1] Literally, "a mouth." The *Jerusalem Bible* translates this "eloquence." Whether the word can be made to reach that far is hard to say. Surely, it at least refers to the ability to speak *well*. In Exodus 4:16; Jeremiah 15:19 "mouth" is used of the effective "spokesman" for another. In these places it seems to be an extension of the idea Jesus had in mind.

he mentioned had to do with content; **spiritual words** had to do with the language in which that teaching was couched. The two were **combined** (the idea being that the two were given by Him side-by-side, the one along with the other[1]). In his commentary on I Corinthians 3:13, Calvin says,

> *The words taught by the Spirit*...are such as are adapted to a pure and simple style, corresponding to the dignity of the Spirit, rather than to an empty ostentation...the power of the Spirit shone forth in it single and unattired without any foreign aid... *sugkrima* is used to mean what is knit together or glued together, and certainly it suits much better Paul's context than *compare* or *liken*, as others have rendered it.

Whether **combined** (as I have rendered it) or *knit* or *glued together* is the more accurate rendering, it is plain that the word's intent is that when the Spirit spoke through the apostles, together with Spirit-given content there was also Spirit-given language. Calvin goes on in the paragraph to speak of the Spirit's *"accommodating* the words to the subject." That is to say, the terminology given by the Spirit exactly fitted the subject matter about which he was inspiring the apostles to speak. The importance of this fact is that the two exactly corresponded to one another.

Why is that important? Because, as every speaker or writer knows, the language choices that one makes when communicating thought will either properly convey his ideas or will distort them. It would have been of little use for God to have given an inerrant revelation through the apostles if He then allowed them, strictly on their own, to determine how best to frame the language that would be used to proclaim that revelation to His church. *Both* had to be absolutely true and accurate or the proc-

---

[1] In modern Greek the term can mean "paralleled."

lamation would have doubtless contained errors. The apostles' own unaided words would have distorted His meaning in various ways.

Language usage has to do with many things, such as accuracy, force, tone and clarity. The Greek word, *sugkrima*, that we have been looking at with some care in order to understand the intention of the Holy Spirit through Paul is therefore significant. To know the import of this word is to understand what was intended; to misunderstand it is to miss it. Language is important. That is why Calvin explained to his reader exactly what the word meant.

Furthermore, proper words used in proper ways are necessary to assure *accuracy*. Preachers are sometimes careless about the language they use in the pulpit. That is probably due to one or both of the following two failures. First, many do not work on enlarging their speaking vocabularies and, therefore, find that they must rely on a minimum of words that is not adequate to cover the vast array of biblical teachings. This fault can easily be remedied if a man wishes to do so. When others are relaxing, giving little thought to how they are expressing themselves in general conversation, the preacher may use such (non-risk) times to think of the very best way to express his ideas. In other words, he will be at work, practicing and improving his working vocabulary and style. Following plans designed by books to increase one's vocabulary is probably not the best way to go about solving the problem. Any man who has graduated from college and seminary already has a reading and recognition vocabulary that is quite sufficient.[1] His problem is not the acquisition of new words. Rather, in most cases the problem is that he has become lax in bringing into his *spoken* vocabulary those terms that he knows already and understands when he *reads* them. That is why he needs to spend time practicing in general conversation. The

---

[1] Sometimes it is too large for normal usage!

same thing is true about learning to structure clear, forceful sentences that exactly express his meaning. He should ask himself from time to time, "now what is the best term or phrase by which to convey my idea?" If he is unsure of the meaning of a word, he should look it up when he has the opportunity to do so, rather than use it inaccurately.

Precision is important when talking about the things of God. But if one's habits of speech in relaxed conversation are sloppy, you can be sure that these habits will bleed over into his speech in the pulpit. That is why a preacher must ever be on the alert, watching his speech at all times. When I refer to sloppy speech, I have in mind the overuse of words like "thing" or the repetitive use of "you know" (that was one of the worst practices spawned in the sixties). These annoying words communicate very little. Precision means that instead of saying "car," one would say "a black '99 BMW." It is a matter of locating and using the word or words that most fittingly describe what it is that you wish to say. Words and phrases that are too general, abstract or vague should be avoided. Saying "car" when you mean "BMW" creates difficulties because the listener is required to fill in what kind of car you have in mind. When he hears the word, he may think of a dented up, broken down Ford from the seventies instead of the shiny, new BMW. If the color black is important to what you are saying, his filling in the color red will lead him astray. It is true, also, that correct word usage and construction of sentences used in general conversation at length will find their way into his sermons.

Now, I don't mean that he ought to be stilted or stuffy in his speech. Attempts to improve by the wrong means often explain why much truth fails to get through to the listener. A preacher's effort to improve in such cases often consists of learning new words, many of which are seldom used in everyday speech. *Koine* Greek (the business Greek of the day) was the Greek in which the New Testament was written and in which the apostles preached. A preacher ought to make it his goal to master the common speech of his day (perhaps best exemplified by the language of the anchors on the nightly newscasts).

Clarity is the second cousin of honesty. Those who want to deceive often find it easiest to use vague or ambiguous language. President Clinton demonstrated how this can be done when he played word games with the terms "is" and "alone." No preacher should be found guilty of using ambiguity in order to deceive— or in order to allow congregants to interpret his words more than one way for fear of their response to the truth, were it more plainly spoken. There is a certain sense of boldness and honesty that clarity communicates to the listener. It is also more persuasive.

How does one achieve clarity? Clarity comes from using simple, everyday, non-technical language.[1] It comes from the use of unambiguous sentences that straightforwardly say what the speaker has in mind. It comes from the avoidance of undue complexity. It comes from the careful choice of words that a speaker knows his audience will interpret properly. It comes also from using biblical terminology, where possible, rather than jargon from Psychology or some other area of life. Paul was concerned about clarity. In Colossians 4:4 he asked the church to pray that he might preach the Word **clearly, as**, he said, he **ought to**. From this we understand that it is not only *desirable but also obligatory* for a preacher to speak clearly.[2] With the apostle, every preacher of the Word should assume this obligation. Those

---

[1] A minimum of technical language, necessary to understand the Bible, should be taught. That means that a preacher will use technical terms *only with explanation*: "…sanctification, putting off the old lifestyle and putting on the new one, …"

[2] It seems that inspiration was not unrelated to human responsibility. Evidently, it was through the means of prayer that God provided this inspiration. The relationship between inspiration and responsibility seems similar to that between God's predestined plan and its outworking through providential circumstances (which He also ordains). Note, later, how boldness in preaching

who ignore it are not worthy of the ministry. While none of us is perfect like the inspiring Spirit, we still must assume the obligation and work at the matter of clarity.

But, as I mentioned, sometimes another factor is related to a lack of clarity. Sometimes preachers are not clear about what the Bible has to say, because they fear the consequences of teaching hard biblical truths. Not everything in the Scriptures sits well with congregations. Yet, the preacher must preach the **whole counsel of God**. He may not hold back anything that God has determined to be **beneficial** to them. That means that frequently the preacher must be **bold** in order to be clear.

Again, note that Paul speaks of boldness as an obligation: **that I may speak boldly, as indeed I *should*** (Ephesians 6:20). Throughout the book of Acts, the preaching of the apostles is characterized as **bold**. The word for boldness that Luke consistently used[1] was *parresia,* which means "freedom to speak without fear of consequences." It is fear, as I said, that often interferes with the clear proclamation of God's truth. But if we would learn anything from the study of the Spirit's work in inspiring preaching, it should be that He gave boldness of speech to the apostles. There is no question about the fact that the Spirit was concerned about bold preaching. In Acts 4, the apostles prayed: **give Your slaves all the boldness needed to speak Your word** (Acts 4:29). In response, we read, **Now as they were praying, the place where they were meeting was shaken and they were all filled with the Holy Spirit and spoke God's word boldly** (Acts 4:31). Undoubtedly, it was the Spirit Who enabled the apostles to be as bold as they were. Were a new generation of preachers to arise who were willing to preach God's

---

was provided by means of prayer. It is true that in ordinary life what has been planned is secured by prayer. Predestination (and inspiration), then, extends to the means; not merely to the end.

[1] There are two Greek words for boldness used in the New Testament. *Parresia* has to do with speech and, therefore, is of special importance to our study.

truth unashamedly and without compromise, we would soon see new power in the church. And the church would make a more forceful impact on the world. Where are the men today who pray for the boldness **necessary** to preach God's Word? That necessity was recognized by the apostles; it must once again be recognized by ministers of the Word!

One of the reasons why there is so little result from preaching is because of the lack of boldness that we have been discussing. There is fear of what Mr. Jones will say or how Mrs. Smith may react. So the preacher tones down what he says, using language that fails to communicate the full force of the passage. God's hatred of sin is termed "displeasure," His call for confession of sin and repentance is made out to be mere apologizing or saying "I'm sorry." He speaks (unbiblically) of God hating the sin and loving the sinner, when he knows full well that it is sinners, not their sin, that God punishes in hell. There is much more of this sort of toning down of the Bible than one might at first realize. Preacher, are you one who has developed the technique? In other cases, the preacher has learned to take the edge off what the Bible teaches by sprinkling his sermon with qualifiers like "some," "often," "frequently," and the like. Consider your present practices.

Words, as the semanticists tell us, are signs. But the preacher ought to recognize that they are also sign*post*s. They point in a particular direction. To call drunkenness a sickness, for instance, points to the physician for the solution; to call it a sin points to Jesus Christ. It is important, therefore, for a preacher to be careful about his terminology lest he wittingly give his congregation wrong directions. Many preachers have learned to use psychological jargon without even thinking about it. How often I have heard men speak of someone having a "guilt complex," when what they meant was guilt![1] If you asked them to define the

---

[1] And even the word "guilt" which itself means culpability (liability to pun-

expression "guilt complex," in most cases they probably could not.

A preacher needs to develop what I like to call "full fluency." Full fluency is the ability to pick out the correct words at high speed and put them together in proper order in sentences that communicate exactly what one wants to say. To be able to do that apart from the inspiration of the Holy Spirit, which we do not have, takes much practice and preparation about which I will speak more fully in the next chapter. For now, let us try to understand full fluency.

Many preachers write out their sermons in full, or nearly so. Some even memorize what they have written. But preaching has to do with the *spoken* word, not the *written* one. Throughout your entire life in the schools, the school marms have done all they could to teach you how to *write* English. While they probably didn't tell you so, they were attempting to get you *not* to write as you speak.[1] You see, written and spoken English are two different things. In writing, you were taught to use an economy of words. You were allowed to use your dictionary not only in order to find the proper spelling of a word, but also to introduce words that you would not ordinarily use in speaking. On and on we could go, pointing out the differences between written and spoken language. But perhaps the best way to approach the subject is to look at it from the perspective of the consumer.

Those who *listen*, unlike those who *read,* encounter different problems, which they solve in very different ways. A reader may read and reread a sentence or paragraph that he does not understand at first. He may reflect upon what he reads by pausing, leaning back in his chair, and thinking about it. If he runs across a term that he does not know, he may pull down the dictionary

---

ishment) has been watered down to refer to the uncomfortable feelings occasioned by guilt.

[1] They may not have realized that this was what the rules they taught were designed to do.

and look it up. He may read a part of an article, go off to work, think about it all day, and then come home at night and take up the matter where he left off. In other words, the writer can expect much more help from the reader than can the speaker from the listener.

The listener must get all the speaker says at the latter's rate (rather than his own), must understand it immediately upon hearing it (he can't ask the speaker to go back and repeat what he just said), and he may not ponder over what is being said or he will miss the rest of the speech. Moreover, he cannot use a dictionary while listening.

What do these differences mean? Well, for the speaker, they mean that he must unlearn much of what the school marms taught him. Instead of an economy of terms, he may have to spread his sentences out a bit, explaining ideas in ways that would never do in a written essay. He may have to repeat hard concepts two or even three times and in various ways for the sake of the listener. Such repetition would be frowned upon by the teacher of written English. He must be careful not to use any technical terms that are not immediately understood by his audience or that he doesn't explain on the spot. On and on we could go, but this is enough to make the point. When Spurgeon's sermons were published on Monday evening following their delivery the day before, it was only after he had spent the morning revising them so as to change them from oral into written form. He knew that unrevised oral English doesn't look good in print. And it shouldn't! The same is true for the reverse: a sermon in written English should sound bad when delivered in oral form.

Now, if a man determines to write out his sermons, he is at a disadvantage. Why? Because for years he has been taught the principles of written language and doesn't have the experience or knowledge of how to write oral English! His written sermons, therefore, most likely will sound stiff and bookish, and will be hard to understand and boring. It is, then, preferable to prepare what one will speak beforehand, noting principal points and key terms or phrases that he deems essential in a *full sentence out-line*.

Why a full sentence outline? For two main reasons. First, if he wants to use the outline in years to come it will be easier for him to understand what he meant from full sentences than from a few words or phrases. Second, until he can say something intelligibly in sentence form, he may be kidding himself about how clearly he understands it.

Moreover, for the sake of clarity, it is important to include at the top of the outline a purpose statement. This should so sharply set forth the purpose of the preacher's sermon that there is no question about what he wishes to achieve. The general purpose will be largely to inform, to convince, or to motivate. When the purpose statement is composed, it should contain one of these three words. Then, along with the general purpose, the rest of the statement should contain the specific purpose. Two examples of a purpose statement might be as follows: I plan to motivate the congregation to give generously to foreign missions; I wish to convince the congregation that predestination is biblical.

I earlier mentioned force and tone as part of language. The former comes from speaking in unambiguous and straightforward language. Definite sentences, not weighted down by qualifications, lend force to one's statements. That is not to say that there is no place for qualifiers. When they are needed, they often are the very best way to achieve accuracy. It would be wrong, for instance, to accuse all Christians of what *some* happen to be doing wrong. The word *some*, therefore, is a necessary qualification. But the tendency to overuse qualifiers is a problem that many weak preachers must overcome.

The use of the second person in speaking is important for directness and force. Too many preachers cast their sermons in the third person mold, while others emphasize the first person.[1]

---

[1] The first person focuses on the preacher rather on God and the congregation.

Both practices are mistakes. You are talking to people—address them directly. A sermon is not a lecture or an essay to which an exhortation is attached. Throughout it is a message from God to His people. He should, therefore, address them directly from the outset and throughout his message. That means that in preaching one usually will use the word "you." If you want to see a good example of how the second person is used effectively, study its use in the Sermon on the Mount.

Of course there will be some third person remarks sprinkled here and there throughout the sermon as it is necessary to explain a passage or concept. But the overall thrust of the message will be to produce some change in the thinking, beliefs or behavior of those who listen. That doesn't usually take place when lecturing.[1] Rather, those who truly care to see change will address their congregations in the second person. The preacher is a messenger from God who has been sent to deliver that message to His people. Preachers should preach to people—not address the angels! Third person preachers tend to preach as if they were tour guides in Palestine. While one may have to take a quick trip to the holy land now and then to make a point, he will always plant his feet on his native soil when preaching.

The tone of a message is a combination of several elements; the two most important are delivery and language. I shall reserve comments on delivery for later. Think now for a bit about tone in terms of language. For one thing, a sermon will be formal or informal depending on the sort of language that one uses. There is nothing stiffly formal about the sermons that you encounter in the New Testament. They impress you as the words of persons passionately concerned about those to whom they are speaking. The speakers come across as persons who want to capture the hearts and lives of their audiences. Their words are those of the man on the street, not those of the polished orator. Paul's com-

---

[1] Third person speaking is the fundamental form of the lecture.

ments in I Corinthians 2 were intended to be a vindication of simple, honest and direct language over against the lectures of the Sophists. And, remember, he spoke the Spirit's words. Listen to what the rulers said:

> Now when they saw the boldness of Peter and John and realized that they were uneducated laymen, they were surprised and recognized that they had been with Jesus.   (Acts 4:13)

It was apparent from their speech that these early preachers had not acquired their speaking ability in the schools; their language was that of the ordinary man. The Spirit used the words of fishermen! The only recognizable acquired traits they exhibited were those that they had learned by spending three and one half years with Jesus (and His language was simple). Yet, their tone was always earnest. They were not up in front of people reciting a piece. They were preaching from their hearts to win the hearts of their listeners. If your tone ever lacks the qualities of earnestness, sincerity and concern, your sermons will suffer accordingly.

Now, word choice will have much to do with tone. If your words are those of the schools, your sermons will suffer. But on the other hand, some words gleaned from the streets may be too debased for the high quality of the message that you are delivering. Your words, while honoring the Name of the One Whose messenger you are, must at the same time communicate to your listeners. The biblical combination that you should emulate might be called a heightened *koine*.[1] The word "guy," for instance, might be common in some quarters, but "person" or "man" would be more appropriate and equally as intelligible. It would be rare to hear the word used on the nightly newscast. On the other hand, for the clause "of which you have heard" it

---

[1] The common language of business, heightened by the subject matter.

would probably be wise to substitute "that you heard about." As Winston Churchill so well put it when replying to those editors who would strike out all prepositions at the conclusion of a sentence, "This is the sort of nonsense up with which I will not put."

Preparation beforehand (mentioned in Mark 13:11; Luke 21:14, 15) was forbidden. The apostles had no need for it. The Spirit provided all that the apostles needed on the spot—exactly when they needed it. But, in mentioning this fact, the Lord was contrasting inspired preaching with what uninspired persons normally do. And that is of importance to you. The preacher today who doesn't think about what he will say or how he will say it *beforehand*, is making a great mistake. And that preparation must extend not only to content, but also to language usage.

Chapter 6

Improving Language Usage

I have already given some hints as to how to improve the use of language in preaching. Uppermost in what I mentioned is the idea of working on improvements in normal life conversations when no one else suspects you are doing so. I said that the improvements you make at such times will bleed over into your preaching. But why? Wouldn't it be better to work on improvements when you are preparing to preach? Absolutely not! And here's why: if you attempt to change your speech habits while you are preaching, or even in conjunction with preparing or rehearsing your sermons, you may discover that you will become far too conscious of what you are doing. It is enough to concentrate on the Lord, the truths that you are teaching, and the response of the congregation—all of which you ought to be doing while preaching. You don't need any distraction that will divert your attention from these all-important matters. Whenever you become concerned about how you are doing what you are doing it makes it more difficult to do it. Take for example the familiar story of the caterpillar that was asked how he walked without getting his many legs tangled up—he couldn't walk once he began to think about it. Something of that sort influencing your preaching can be devastating.

So, if working on the changes that you wish to make are best carried on outside of the pulpit, what is the best plan to follow? Well, I suggest a two-pronged effort. First, whenever you are in non-crucial conversations—especially when relaxed with family or friends—take special care about how you speak. Introduce new phrases, words or sentence structures into your speech. If you have a particular improvement in view, work on it over a period of time until the change has taken place, and you feel perfectly comfortable using it without much of a conscious effort. Don't be discouraged if at first you find it difficult to develop new habitual patterns of speech; it will probably take at least six weeks of regular effort in order to replace older patterns with new ones. Don't give up.

The second half of the improvement plan is working on telling a brief story every day. As you drive home from the church, rehearse the story for yourself. You should practice telling it out loud in the car (your shiny, black '99 BMW? Ha!). Do so until you think that you have mastered the best way possible to tell it. Then, around the supper table, tell the story for your family. The story should be about something that happened that day, or something that you read about. Again, persist at this for as long as you are working on some particular improvement. You will, of course, introduce that improvement into the story each evening until it becomes a part of your normal repertoire—that is, "second nature" to you.

In both of these methods of improvement you want to be sure that you don't work on too many items at once. I would suggest that you work on no more than two or three improvements at any one time. Otherwise, you may discover that *no* improvement is being made. It is better to concentrate your efforts and improve slowly but surely. Master a few items, *then* move on to a few more.

Let's take an example or two. Suppose that you are concerned about a grammatical matter. You have had your attention called to the fact that you wrongly use the phrase "you and I." You habitually say such things as, "He asks you and I…" You have learned that the easy way to know what to say is to drop the first part of the phrase ("you and") while retaining the second ("I"). You'd never say, "He asks I." You'd always say, "He asks me." Now, add on the words that you dropped: "He asks you and me." So, in conversations, stories around the table, you will introduce sentences in which you will be forced to choose between "I" or "me." Having done so for several weeks, you should have no problem with the construction in the future; it will have become a natural part of your speech. Then, without making any conscious choices when preaching, you will find yourself speaking in a grammatically correct manner. Indeed, you will forget all about working on the problem when you get up to preach. So what if, for the first few weeks, while practicing during conversations and the telling of stories, you continue to murder the King's English! You've been doing so for years— what's a couple more weeks? In time, if you keep working outside the pulpit, you will discover that your practice will change when in the pulpit. You may not even become conscious of the change when it takes place, but the school teachers in the congregation will let you know—just as they originally told you how the wrong use of "you and I" offended their ears.

Now, tone is another matter. Here, you should probably do some conscious pre-planning. There may be particular words that you wish to use. If you write these key words into the outline, you will then be able to use them during the message. If you have been communicating weakness by the overuse of concessive words like "I think," "some believe," "perhaps," "it would seem" and the like, stop using them. How? When speaking informally, whenever you use one of these unnecessarily, have your wife alert you. Write into the outline, instead, terms like, "God says," "The Bible teaches," "Without a doubt." Learn to replace those weak qualifiers with these stronger ones. Soon your preaching will take on the new tone of certainty and assurance.

Tone also is communicated by the kinds of nouns and verbs you choose. If you are used to saying "it is thought," change that to an active verb: "I think." If you are in the habit of overworking abstract nouns like "things," then state exactly what those things are. An example of this might be, "There are a number of things wrong with this church that it's time that we straightened up." Well, if you expect the congregation to shape up, you'd better tell them what "things" you have in mind. Moreover, you may have relatively small things in mind (painting, mowing the grass, cleaning the carpet), and they may fill in the meaning of "things" with larger ones (fights between members, laxness on the part of the elders, sinful affairs)—and become incensed. Be definite by using concrete nouns like "BMW" instead of "car"!

Colorful verbs and nouns also help. The sky you are describing was not merely "bright"—it was "radiant" or "aglow." Moreover, as you looked at it you were not only "impressed" with it, you were deeply "moved" within. The Israelites didn't just "win" the war, they "massacred" the enemy. God is not merely "great"; He is "awe-inspiring." Choose the more expressive term wherever possible. With reference to this last overworked word, "great," there is a dangerous pit into which many preachers plummet. They have a tendency to call everything "great." Then, when they come to something that deserves the appellation, they don't know how to express it. Many times they end up saying something like "this is really great," or even "really, really great!" If it is great, it is great. If something isn't *really* great, it isn't great at all. Reserve superlatives for those rare occasions on which they accurately express a truly unusual place, situation, person, or event.

Then, there is the problem of the word "unique." That which is unique is one of a kind. It lends itself to no degrees. Something cannot be "really" unique or "most" unique. If a girl is pregnant, she is pregnant. She couldn't be said to be *really* pregnant, *most* pregnant, or *almost* pregnant. She is either pregnant or she isn't. Similarly, something is either unique or it isn't. And, whenever the word unique is used, it should be used with care, making sure that what you are describing is truly the only one of its kind. It is proper to describe Jesus as the unique Son of God; but unless the program at church that you are announcing is the only one like it that has ever been conducted, don't call it unique. It may be unusual or different, but not unique.

When trying to overcome bad habits, in which the goal is to eliminate some unwanted expression (e.g., the repetitive, non-communicative use of "you know"), it is probably best to enlist the aid of another person. If you tell your wife to signal you every time she hears you reiterating the offensive "you know," that will help you (1) to become aware of how frequently you use it (creating a greater desire to change) (2) to say what you are trying to say in a more acceptable way—on the spot. When the two of you are at home alone, perhaps, you could ask your wife to use a response signal like, "Know? I don't know. Why don't you tell me?" Of course, she could not do that in the company of others. The signal that you devise to use in those circumstances ought to be undetectable by others (a wink, a hand motion, a cough or something similar). Perhaps you want to begin the effort *only* at home at first, especially if there is any question about how best to pull off signaling elsewhere.

In thinking about the right language to use, one could consider many things; but above all, the key to good language is that it communicates the truth of God without addition or subtraction and without calling attention to itself.

Chapter 7

The Spirit's Third Concern

True, Jesus mentioned wisdom only once in the four references that we have cited (in Luke 21:14, 15). But if the Lord says something once it is not necessary for us to have Him say it again. The third concern of the Holy Spirit in preaching is the practical application of the truth to life—wisdom. That this is the force of the word is apparent from the way it is used in Proverbs and Ecclesiastes in the Old Testament, as well as in James in the New. In the Luke passage Jesus says, "I will give you words (a mouth) and wisdom that none of your opponents will be able to withstand or contradict." The thrust of the word **wisdom** seems to be that in your preaching style—the ways in which you handle revelation in relationship to your listeners—you will triumph over all objections, making your point persuasively. That is not to say that they will all believe, or even respond favorably. But some will. And all will be obligated to acknowledge that what you have said is effective—whether they do so audibly or not. The personal, relational factor is prominent in the passage. Jesus was speaking about wisdom in relation to people.

The Lord spoke of His servants becoming **wise as snakes** (Matthew 10:16[1]) in the context of His sending them out among wolves[2] (v. 16). Significantly, it was in that very context that He promised that their preaching would be inspired by the Spirit (vv. 19, 20). The snake is considered crafty. He knows when to strike and when to slither away. The word "crafty" can have

---

[1] I have dealt with the other half of the verse ("harmless as doves") in my book *Maintaining the Delicate Balance*, pp. 1-4 (*q.v.*).
[2] There are still wolves among the flock. Wisdom also has to do with how to deal with them.

59

good or bad connotations. Here, of course, it has good ones. The idea is that they were to be clever and resourceful, able to stand up against opposition in ways that would astound those who opposed. So it is clear that Jesus' concern, as was that of the Spirit, was to produce *clever* preaching. But that must be understood properly. The cleverness that He had in mind was always non-manipulative. It involved wise responses, telling assertions, and powerful questions.

The Spirit's third concern, then, had to do with the *manner* in which the message is presented. And the manner of presentation grows out of the preacher's *relationship to the audience*. In every preaching event the following human elements are always present: the preacher, the message, and the congregation (of course God is also there, but He is at work in all three). Manner has to do with how these three elements are related. It therefore involves the ethos of the speaker, the knowledge, prejudices and spiritual condition of the people, and the way in which the preacher presents the message. The proper relationship of these three elements is what the Spirit called **wisdom** in preaching.

To get at this a little more concretely, consider the sermon by Stephen. This sermon was not a failure, even though the preacher was stoned to death. He was preaching under the power of the Spirit (Acts 7:55). This was a hostile crowd if there ever was one. But Stephen was able to preach at length before he was stopped by them. How was that? The Spirit wisely led him to preach inductively. What does that mean? In a deductive message one states his main thesis at the outset, then throughout the message gives the supporting arguments for it. But in an inductive message the preacher begins with particulars, gradually gathering them together to reach an irresistible conclusion. Had Stephen preached deductively, he would not have been able to speak more than a line or two before the crowd would have turned on him. But by preaching inductively—the thing to do with a hostile crowd—he was able to establish all he intended before coming to his conclusion. That was, as Stifler put it (when writing about Peter's Pentecostal sermon), a "piece of bright wisdom." Where did it come from? From the Holy Spirit. So we see that the wisdom of the Spirit is connected with the structure of the message.

Paul is also an example of wise, healthy, biblical flexibility. This flexibility enabled him to adapt without compromise to every sort of audience and circumstance that one could imagine. It is one of the Spirit's concerns in the book of Acts to demonstrate how the Gospel is adaptable to all. The record of Paul's preaching in Acts shows how to alter form and presentation without changing substance. He knew when to speak and when not to. Before the Sanhedrin, for instance, he was aware that he would not get a fair hearing (Acts 23). So, instead of delivering a message before them, he threw the golden apple into their midst and watched them squabble over it.[1] That was wise. Every time that Jesus or the other apostles had been brought before this kangaroo court they had failed to receive justice. He would not receive it either. Paul knew his audience (after all, in the past he had worked closely with them[2]).

Paul stood before the Athenian philosophers and the members of the Council of the Areopagus and trapped them by their own ignorance into hearing his message about the "unknown god."[3] Some have thought that he was unsuccessful here since no church is said to have been established. This they attribute to the way that he preached. They think that he overadapted to this sophisticated audience.

---

[1] He raised the question of the resurrection. The Pharisees believed in it; the Sadducees did not. Paul knew that his remark would raise a conflict among them.

[2] Their initial treatment of him showed that he would not be treated fairly (cf. Acts 23:2).

[3] The council of the Areopagus had condemned Socrates to death for setting forth new gods. This was the same charge that some were trying to bring

Just the opposite is true. If you preached at Harvard University on one occasion and at the conclusion of your message had a convert from among the trustees, a prominent woman who professed faith, a number of students who believed and an invitation to come again to speak, wouldn't you think that your afternoon had been well spent? That is the equivalent of what happened in Athens. It is foolishness to think that Paul made a mistake![1] Moreover, such thinking comes from a failure to recognize that the Spirit was in control, giving Paul the **words and wisdom** to speak. This wisdom commanded the respect of the crowd. Wisdom in preaching, then, may have much to do with the structure of the message and with the manner in which the audience is captured and made to listen.

Do all of your sermons look alike? Well, if so, you need to work on the approach that you use in relating to the congregation. If they are largely in agreement with what you will say, speak deductively. Then you can hammer the main points home again and again throughout the message. If hostile, use an inductive approach as Stephen did. If there is something in the circumstance that can be turned to an advantage (as Paul did at Athens), then use it as a lead into the message. If the occasion calls for a catalyst to bring division to the fore, then toss the golden apple into their midst.

You do not preach to bland faces. You must preach to *people* of *various* sorts. It is true that people in the average congregation

---

against Paul (Acts 17:18, 19). Paul would have none of this. He challenged them to convict him, since they, themselves, had erected an altar "to an unknown god." He was simply telling them about the God that they professed not to know. This striking introduction was nothing less than the Holy Spirit's **wisdom**. The Holy Spirit thereby showed that His wisdom was superior to that of the philosopher Socrates! Doubtless, there were some who heard who chuckled and said to one another, "Well, I guess that he got us there, didn't he?"

[1] With such a distorted view of biblical sermons, no wonder men fail to study and learn from them.

differ—sometimes greatly. Some are older, some younger. Some are new converts, some mature Christians. Some have one interest, some another. Some are filled with certain prejudices, some with opposite ones. How do you analyze such a congregation so as to adapt to it? That is a fair question. The answer is found in Revelation 2 and 3. In those two chapters the Lord Jesus analyzes each of the seven congregations. He speaks about each *as a whole.*[1] It is as if He accorded to each congregation a personality of its own. One is rich, but poor; another poor, but rich. You must do the same. You cannot speak to everyone in particular. But you can take the temper of a congregation and address it as if it were one person—the way that Jesus did. That is possible because each congregation does exhibit a personality of its own. Perhaps it is alive, but dying. Perhaps it is riddled with unbelief or apathy. Possibly it is located in an area where there is great opportunity if only it would enter into it. Possibly it is sour and cynical about most things. What is the personality and the spiritual condition of the congregation to which you regularly preach? If you cannot characterize it well, you probably don't exercise much wisdom in how you approach it from week to week or how you structure your messages. It is time to engage in some wise analysis. The idea, then, is to begin with people where they are.

Often events that have recently transpired provide an avenue of approach. Remember how Jesus spoke of the Galileans on whom the tower fell? Well, He used that to teach the truth that all alike are sinners. Paul's use of the altar that he had recently viewed when walking through the streets of Athens became the springboard for his message (as well as for his acquittal of any charge of proclaiming an unlicensed religion in the city). It takes wisdom to preach. Remember, wisdom is the practical use of truth. Wise preaching presents truth in a manner calculated to get

---

[1] In some cases, he divides the congregation into two sections.

the message across to a particular audience. Do you pray that the Spirit will give you wisdom in the preparation and delivery of a message?

Once when Chrysostom was preaching, the lamplighters came into the auditorium. The congregation was distracted by them. How did Chrysostom handle that? He stopped what he was saying and declared, "You are watching the lamplighters, but I am lighting a lamp from God's Word!" He wisely gave them a chance to get the distraction "out of their systems" and then turned the incident into an opportunity to teach spiritual truth. Interruptions can be advantageous. A crying baby causing a ruckus may be quite distracting (and embarrassing to the parents). The wise preacher might smile and say, "Ah. Out of the mouth of babes and sucklings—" and then make the point that Jesus did on the occasion when He uttered those words.

In Pisidian Antioch Paul was quite aware of the presence of many God-fearers (Gentiles who believed in Yahweh, but had not fully become Jews) in the congregation (Acts 13:16). Throughout his message he kept them in mind. Even the manner in which he taught was an attempt to appeal to them (standing while preaching—a Greek way of teaching—rather than using the seated posture of the Jews). And, while addressing the Jews, he didn't fail to mention these God-fearers as well. Consequently, at the conclusion of his message he had even more converts from the Gentiles than from the Jews.

So wisdom in preaching has many dimensions. In all of them there is something that relates especially to the congregation that is being addressed. That seems to be the dominant factor. Preaching is, therefore, specialized. Messages ought, in some manner or other, to be particularized. A lecturer appropriately may give the same lecture over and over again from place to place in exactly the same words. A preacher is a fool if he does this (either that, or he isn't preaching; he too is lecturing). Even if most of the message is the same (as indeed it was in the case of

Paul), in one way or another it ought to be adapted. In the book of Acts there was no alteration of the basic message either by diminution or embellishment, but there was much adaptation. **Wisdom** in preaching so alters the approach to a congregation that the *same* message is proclaimed in a *particularized* manner. And remember, that is done by finding something in each preaching situation relating to that congregation that helps relate the message.

There are times to use a rod and there are times to be very gentle in one's preaching (cf. I Corinthians 4:13, 14, 20, 21); but the purpose in preaching to God's people must always be for edification (building people up; II Corinthians 10:8; 13:10). It should never be vindictive (tearing them down). Wisdom also involves knowing when to use the rod and when to use gentleness. Paul knew when to leave a situation to give the church an opportunity to change in ways that would solve their problems, and when to come and set things straight (cf. III John 12). This he did in relationship to the Corinthian church. And, knowing the people there, he got good results. The same sort of judgment about when to rebuke, when to back off, when to gently persuade, and so on, was a large part of the wisdom that the Spirit provided. Many preachers get themselves in trouble unnecessarily by failing to use wisdom in rebuking and encouraging their congregations. Yet that is clearly a large part of preaching— knowing when to come down hard and when to let up a bit.

Since preaching is relational, it involves personal elements. The personalities of the members of the audience, their spiritual growth, and their knowledge of the Scriptures are all significant when determining what, when, and how to preach. The personality of the preacher is also involved. If a congregation loves its preacher, he will probably be able to preach most anything from the Bible without fear of retaliation. If, on the other hand, his rating is questionable—or very low—anything he says (even of the most innocent sort) may be misconstrued by members of the congregation. So, part of having wisdom is determining one's standing with the congregation. If it is questionable (or worse), the preacher may have to do whatever is necessary to change that situation. Otherwise, he will be unable to deal with issues pertinent to the church. They will not hear what he has to say until they are ready to listen to him. On the other hand, if the attitude of the congregation is merely apathetic, the preacher may have to raise the interest level of the congregation before he is able to impart other vital truths that they obviously need to hear. In other words, there is the message, and there is the messenger; there is the message, and there are the recipients. All three must be in line before preaching can be widely successful. It is important, then, for the preacher to evaluate such matters if he is to preach with wisdom.

When the relational factors (including the relationships of the preacher and the congregation with God) are in basic harmony a preacher will enjoy great freedom in preaching. This freedom will extend to both his choice of subject manner and the manner in which he presents it. But when relationships are bad,[1] far more concern about both must be taken to assure that the message gets through in spite of the disharmony. Often a preacher must wait to deliver certain truths until first the relational matters are dealt with. It will take wisdom to discern such things. Some men, lacking wisdom, fail to take such matters into consideration. Instead of seeking the wisest way, they just stumble and bumble ahead. Wisdom is essential. If a preacher doesn't have it and doesn't care to or cannot attain it, he should reconsider his call to the ministry. This is not an optional matter at all.

---

[1] Every preacher needs some elder in his congregation who will be utterly frank about such matters. If he gets an unfavorable report, he will be wise to call the rest of the elders together and discuss the matter (and what, if anything, can be done about it) before the matter deteriorates any further. This elder must be utterly trustworthy and must himself have the wisdom to assess matters rightly.

Pastorates are destroyed more often from lack of wisdom in preaching and otherwise relating to people than from doctrinal differences. If you don't have wisdom, ask God for it. Remember what James wrote:

> So if any of you lacks wisdom, let him ask God for it, since He gives to everyone unreservedly and without reproaching, and it will be given to him. But let him ask in faith, without doubting, because a person who doubts is like a wave of the sea and tossed by the wind. That person shouldn't suppose that he will receive anything from the Lord, because a double-minded person is unstable in all his ways.
>
> (James 1:5-8)

The upshot of those words is that if a man called by God and gifted in other ways lacks wisdom, it is his fault—not God's. He must confess his sin; he must recognize that he either has not because he asks not (James 4:2), or because he asks lacking faith. He must believe God and take Him at His Word. He can experience a new ministry that is based not merely on academic prowess, but on the wisdom that comes from above (cf. James 3:17, 18).

So, it is important always to observe carefully the attitudes of a congregation's members, their approaches to truth, and the actions that you have seen among them before determining the approach that you will use in preparing and preaching any given message.

Chapter 8
On Obtaining Wisdom

"If, as James says, wisdom is obtained by asking for it, what is this chapter all about? Don't I simply have to pray?" Whoa! Not so fast. Like many places in the Bible, some promises express only part of the picture. One might try to say the same thing about the request, **Give us this day our daily bread**, in the Lord's prayer; He could reason, "All I have to do is pray and it will appear each day—right?" Wrong! Paul says (II Thessalonians 3:10) that if a person won't work he shouldn't eat. That, you see, is the other side of the issue.[1] And consider Christ's prayer from the cross, **"Father, forgive them, for they know not what they do."** Was that prayer ever answered? Well, if you are wondering, let me tell you that it was. It was answered on the Day of Pentecost and on those occasions immediately thereafter when Peter preached to the very persons who crucified Jesus (cf. Acts 3:12-15). But the prayer was answered by the use of human means, not apart from them. That is to say, in order to be forgiven the Jews had to hear the gospel, repent of their sins and believe in the Lord Jesus Christ as Savior.[2]

In addition, when James says that God liberally gives wisdom without reproaching those who ask,[3] he is spelling out only one aspect of acquiring wisdom; he isn't telling the whole story. "How do you know that?" you may ask. Because elsewhere the

---

[1] The prayer, in effect, means, "Lord, give me the strength, the ability and the opportunity to work for my daily bread." Of course, in emergency situations, God might provide the bread through someone else. But so long as one is able to earn his bread, he must pray *and* work for it. Prayer doesn't preclude work.

[2] Romans 10:14 applies to this situation, as it does to others.

[3] "Why didn't you think to ask sooner?" or something of the sort.

Scriptures tell us that wisdom is acquired through human effort—just like daily bread. That is often the way it is with matters about which we are to pray: prayer becomes the background for action. It is the way in which we ask God to enable us to do whatever it is that He has told us to do. We can't acquire wisdom by prayer alone (as Solomon did); nor can we obtain it without prayer. The Spirit makes that possible through the means that He has determined.

"Well, then, what is the means by which one obtains wisdom?" That question is easily answered. Listen to Solomon himself:

> The proverbs of Solomon, David's son, king of Israel—To know wisdom and disciplined training; to understand words of discernment; to receive disciplined training in prudence, right living, judgment and uprightness. To give clear perception to the naive, knowledge and discretion to the young man.
>
> (Proverbs 1:1-4)

In this introduction to the book of Proverbs the writer explains why the book was written and what it can do for the sympathetic reader. Notice, at the top of the list of things that Proverbs supplies for those who will learn from it is **wisdom**. Indeed, some think that wisdom is mentioned first because the rest of the items listed are but a part or extension of wisdom.

Surely, the books called "Wisdom literature" (Job, Proverbs, Ecclesiastes and James) were not included in the Bible merely to show us what such wisdom entails. They do that of course. But, as Proverbs makes clear, they were written primarily to help us *become* wise. So, a preacher may obtain wisdom through the prayerful study and application of the Scriptures—in particular, but not exclusively, through the assimilation of the teaching found in the wisdom books mentioned above. While it isn't possible to cover all the biblical wisdom materials, we might at least look at some of those things that are said in the wisdom books that would point a preacher in the right direction.

Of course (and this should not be necessary to mention), Proverbs 9:10 makes salvation *the* fundamental prerequisite: **The fear of Yahweh is the beginning of wisdom**. That is where it all begins. Perhaps a word or two ought to be said about the words "the fear of Yahweh." Often, as in the Berkeley version, the word "fear" is translated "reverence." While there surely is that element in the word, it is doubtful whether the term "reverence" entirely encompasses the concept of "fear." The ordinary word for fear is used. And when you note the use of "fear" in Psalm 2:11, you cannot fail to see that in the parallelism of the verse it is connected with "trembling": **Worship Yahweh in fear, and rejoice with trembling**. While the word doesn't denote terror on the part of the believer, it has connotations of the sort of awe that made the people of Israel withdraw trembling from God's manifestation of Himself on Mount Sinai (Exodus 20:18-21). This idea of *trembling* needs further explanation.

I used to have a dog of the akita breed named Frisco. Though he was gentle with children and those he knew, he was very intimidating to others—and to other dogs! My son's dog, General, lives next door. From his looks you'd think he'd be more than a match for Frisco. But General hardly lives up to his name. He is a lovable dog that even hesitates when you want to pet him. Well, Frisco at times would bully General. He would tear across the lawn and knock General over. In those cases, General would turn over on his back, exposing himself in a totally vulnerable way and tremble. It is said that fear leads to a flight or fight response. It seems to me that analysis is insufficient. There is a third response as well: pure fright. There is a pleading for mercy, a making of one's self vulnerable, and a submitting of one's self to another that expresses something of what this third response is like. It would seem that the word "fear" in expressions that relate to God has something of that element in it. It is a submitting to God by faith. It is making one's self vulnerable to the One Who is so far superior in glory and might that it can only make him tremble as he thinks of the dazzling power that He wields. This humble submission to God is **the beginning of wisdom**.

What, beyond its **beginning**, may one learn about wisdom for preaching? First, there is the general understanding of man that is delineated in the Scriptures—and especially in the wisdom books. This understanding of man is essential to relating properly to people in various sorts of congregations. Wisdom is not necessary when approaching each audience identically (as the lecturer does). In preaching one is never merely informative (though, as we have seen, that may be the major emphasis of some sermons). The faithful preacher is out to change the lives of those to whom he delivers God's message of transformation. So, he will wisely *adapt* what he has to say and how he says it to each group and in each situation.

In the seven letters to the seven churches that are addressed in the book of Revelation, Jesus approached each church uniquely. To Ephesus, He was One involved with the stars and the lampstands (Revelation 2:1); to Smyrna, He was the Beginning and the End, and the resurrected One (Revelation 2:8); to the church in Pergamos He was the One with the broadsword (Revelation 2:12); to the church at Thyatira, He appeared as God's Son with eyes of fire and feet of brass (Revelation 2:18); to the church of Sardis He was the One with the seven spirits and the stars (Revelation 3:1); to the church at Philadelphia He was the Genuine One Who had the key of David (Revelation 3:7); and to the church of Laodicea He appeared as the Amen, the faithful Witness and the Ruler of God's creation (Revelation 3:14). Was it only for the sake of variety that Jesus made Himself known to each of these churches in a different way? Of course not. In His perfect wisdom, Jesus confronted each with the aspect(s) of Himself that was exactly appropriate.[1] It is that sort of wisdom that a good preacher knows how to exercise. And he learns it first and foremost from the descriptions of men and congregations that he encounters in the Bible. Having discovered that a church to which he must preach is similar to the one at Corinth, Colossae or Philippi, he will learn much about the needed approach to such a congregation from the preacher who wrote to those churches. As he discovers what some of the persons in these congregations were like, he will also learn much from how the biblical preachers dealt with those who had similar problems (cf. Philippians 1:12-2:13, 4:1-3).

But much of his wisdom will simply be fallout that comes from his prayerful reading of the wisdom books. For instance, he will not fail to notice that the Preacher searched to find just the right words (Ecclesiastes 12:10). That will encourage him to be careful about the language he uses. From Proverbs 15:1 he will learn to use gentleness in speaking to those who have been saying harsh (literally, "painful") things. Many preachers, not heeding this wisdom from Solomon, blunder ahead, starting full-fledged wars in their congregations. He will also discover in the very next verse that he ought to speak in such a way that what he says will seem "acceptable" (literally, "good") to those who listen. Proverbs 15:23 speaks about the joy that is involved in an "apt answer," and the delight that a "timely word" brings. He will spend time studying the tenth chapter of Proverbs in which he finds so much about speech and its effects. But I could go on and on. Instead, I shall list some of the passages in Proverbs that he ought to study in order to improve his approach to people in preaching. They do not address the problem of preaching specifically, but all of them involve speech and are pertinent to the preaching situation. They are as follows:

---

[1] We cannot explicate this point here. Consult the commentaries. But, for example, compare Revelation 2:12 with 2:16.

Proverbs 2:6; 4:24 (important for those who use canned illustrations as if they were their own, etc.); 6:12 (ditto); 8:6-9 (exemplary for every preacher); 10:11; 10:19 (for those who don't know when to stop); 10:20, 21; 10:31; 12:18 (important in times of controversy); 15:4 (for those with sharp tongues); 15:7; 15:28 (important for those who speak too hastily); 16:21 (note especially the second half of the verse); 16:23, 24; 17:27; 18:4; 18:20 (how a preacher earns his living); 18:21 (how he may quickly lose it, and how crucial an activity preaching is); 20:15 (how valuable wise speech is); 21:23 (a preacher must be careful about what he says, how he says it and his approach in doing so); 24:26 (what happens when you really help others through solid preaching); 27:2 (be careful about intruding yourself into your sermons).

I have slightly annotated some of the above references, not to indicate that these are the only helpful insights that one may learn from them, but simply as suggestions about the import these verses might have. Obviously, my comments have only to do with speech itself. Other insights that the verses offer about human beings will help preachers too. But if someone has to start somewhere in his search for wisdom, it might be just as well that he begin with those verses that tell him something directly about speaking. After all, speech is the preacher's stock-in-trade.

I could go on. One last note, however. Remember, even if you have pastored a congregation for many years, it is ever changing. It is important to assess and then reassess the congregation frequently. Otherwise you may be preaching to a congregation as it used to be instead of what it now has become. With that final word, let us turn to the fourth concern of the Holy Spirit.

Chapter 9
The Spirit's Fourth Concern

When Jesus told the disciples that the Spirit would inspire their preaching, He emphasized that this divinely-given ability to say the right things in the right words and in the right manner would be granted at the *right time.* That is to say, the apostles would receive what they needed *at the moment when they needed it.* He was concerned with timeliness. Listen to His words:

> ... what you must say will be given to you *in that hour*
> (Matthew 10);

> ... say whatever is given to you *in that hour*
> (Mark 13);

> ... the Holy Spirit will teach you *in that very hour* what you ought to say (Luke 12).

There can be no doubt that when the apostles preached they were never at a loss for words. It is one of the amazing things in the book of Acts that untrained men like Peter and Stephen, for instance, responded with such penetrating wisdom and truth to those who questioned them. The very fact that truth, in appropriate words to communicate it, was there on their lips as they proclaimed it, shows how these prophecies were fulfilled. They never hesitated or stumbled over their words. The Spirit gave them exactly what they needed precisely when they needed it. What a boon to their preaching! Preacher, wouldn't you like to have that ability today?

Well, it is altogether possible *by hard work* for you to approximate to a great extent what the Spirit did for them with *no effort* on their part whatsoever. Indeed so far from putting forth effort, they were not even to be *concerned* about what they would say (each of the citations of the promise mentions this fact. The Luke 21 reference goes so far as to discourage even any prior *practice* of their defenses—a means of improvement that every good, uninspired speaker has found helpful). But, while approaching non-hesitancy, and even full fluency at times, the uninspired preacher will never be entirely ready to speak the exact words that he ought to speak on every occasion.

Consider your own preaching. How many times have you found yourself after a message wishing you had said something more, something else or something different? How often have you later thought, "I wish I had put that point a bit differently? Perhaps, if I had switched the first and the second points...." Did you ever said to yourself, "I guess I wasn't as clear (or thoughtful, or careful) as I might have been. I wish I could preach that message all over again!"? Possibly you chafed at the bit until you *did* get that opportunity—at some other church perhaps. But then, having made the alterations you wished, possibly you noticed some further changes you ought to have made. And on and on it goes.[1] The trouble is that you can never go back and do it over again. Once preached, that message to that group on that occasion is finished—for good! Preaching it over again differently is one thing that the apostles never had the slightest need to do; when they preached, they always got it right the *first* time. And they never had regrets like those expressed above.

---

[1] If nothing like this has ever happened to you it is possible that you are not nearly as self-critical as you ought to be. You may need to rethink your sermon evaluation process. Of course, if you have no such process in place, it will be time to develop one. Whatever process you eventually set in place, you should be sure that it involves the four concerns of the Holy Spirit. If this book does nothing more for you than to etch out those four concerns so that you will determine to regularly examine your preaching in the light of them, it will have achieved much of its purpose. You should be able to see definite improvement in each of the four areas each year or something is wrong.

Well, surely you can begin to work on timeliness since this is an obvious concern of the Holy Spirit. How many messages are impaired by our deficiencies? How many of those deficiencies could have been avoided? How many of them come from the inability to say the right thing in the right way *at the right time*? How can you learn to do better in the future? Those are the concerns that every preacher *ought* to have.

At this point, it might be useful to look at some of the reasons why we aren't more articulate in the pulpit. The following might be a check list against which you can evaluate yourself:[1]

1. Have you spent adequate *time* preparing for the message?
2. Do you know exactly what the *purpose* of the message is?
3. Are you sure of your *exegesis*?
4. Does *fear* of consequences hinder you when you preach?
5. Have you been *working* on improving your language capabilities?
6. Do you *know* your congregation as you ought to?
7. Have you *adapted* your message to the present personality of the congregation?
8. Have you developed adequate *illustrations* to clarify difficult truths?
9. Are you *excited* about what you have to say?
10. Have you opted for a deductive or *inductive* approach for good reasons?
11. Does your full sentence *outline* hold together and progress properly?
12. Will your *introduction* grip the congregation?
13. Does your *conclusion* exhort the congregation to fulfill the purpose in view?
14. Have you *practiced* the sermon beforehand?

---

[1] It might be well to copy off this list of items, along with any additional factors you might find helpful, and put it under glass on your desk. Conceivably you could check out these items when preparing messages and when you are evaluating the tapes of them after they have been preached.

15. Have you underlined *key* words and phrases you want to be sure to use?
16. Will you have it videotaped for further *evaluation* leading to improvement?
17. When viewing the tape, what needed *improvements* do you discern?
18. Do you *know* how to make those improvements?
19. Did you use the COLD SOAP *grid* to help you relate preaching elements to factors?
20. Are the four *concerns* of the Spirit also those that concern you?

While these 20 questions are neither exhaustive nor specifically focused on your individual needs for evaluation and improvement, their general nature makes them applicable to every preacher. I would suggest that if one or more of them is especially pertinent to your preaching that you highlight it with a yellow or orange felt tip pen. In that way, while you are using the list to make a general evaluation of your preaching practices you will not forget to take a special look at the item that you have highlighted.

Timeliness involves appropriateness as well as the ability to deal with something without undue hesitation. What I mean is that whatever the immediate situation, you will know just how to adjust and speak tellingly to it. No two preaching situations are ever the same. If nothing else, each has its own peculiar nuances. Good preachers have learned to adjust in a timely way to each. I mentioned how Chrysostom used the distraction of the lamplighters as a means of emphasizing what he was saying. That is one way in which timeliness is achieved—by adapting to changes that occur during the sermon itself.

I remember when delivering the Griffith Thomas lectures on counseling at Dallas Theological Seminary I was using an illustration that included a person by the name of Fred. Inadvertently, I said "Freud" when I meant "Fred." The seven hundred or so persons in attendance broke into laughter. I was thankful that it lasted for a while since that time lag gave me an opportunity to think. How would I bring them back to me? Suddenly, the answer came to my mind, just as the laughter was subsiding. I continued, "Sorry, that was a Freddian slip!" That did the trick. After additional longer and more intense laughter, I was able to continue with their good will. I haven't often been able to do things like that, but this was a joyous exception. I wish I could do that sort of thing all the time. It would help make up for the many defects in my preaching that I continue to detect. Notwithstanding, I use this example simply to show you what I mean by the word "appropriateness." The appropriate word at exactly the right time can be most helpful. Think about how bad I would have felt if that response had occurred to me only after I sat down, having been embarrassed by my *faux pas*!

How do you plan ahead for such responses? You really can't. But you can create a sort of mentality in yourself that helps you to snap back in a situation that needs reclaiming. What is such a mentality like, and how do you go about obtaining this wit and wisdom? One thing that you can do is to engage in a good bit of friendly banter with others you trust. What I mean is to lightly play around with language in relaxed conversations with your friends. Friendly repartee also is of great value in the learning process.

Many claim that they don't like puns. But the more loudly they groan at your puns, the more they probably appreciate them. The conventional "sophisticated" response to a pun is to groan. But puns are useful (along with other ways you may play around with language) and probably the easiest place to begin your work. I think that the "Freddian slip" response was just that—a sort of conventional way that I had learned to respond from punning with others in general conversations.

At any rate, the whole idea of thrust-and-response in conversation (repartee) is useful to engage in so long as it remains playful and friendly. I emphasize this because sometimes if you aren't careful, it can become a matter of one-upmanship or even bitter rivalry. And that is exactly what should not happen. That can hurt your friends and can tempt you to develop the wrong repertoire of responses. Moreover, it can encourage a mindset in which you think that you must always win the word battles that you engage in, rather than enjoying the apt responses of others as well as your own. So pick your friends and situations, and work hard to develop your ability to respond rapidly and wittily.

There are other ways to develop the capacity to respond to circumstances in which you may find yourself. I am thinking now of those circumstances in which you know beforehand that you will be on the spot and quick responses will be required of you. Here, preparation—at least of a last minute sort—will be possible. Take the last minute prepared response first. Often you will be asked to speak only at the conclusion of a dinner. Remarks which you make grow out of something that you saw or heard during the dinner itself are better than the canned after dinner quips that everyone has heard before and certainly doesn't want to hear again. To do this sort of thing well means that you will be thinking hard about the matter while you are eating. You will be listening to what others say, and you will be watching what is going on. All the while you will be searching for that appropriate, timely remark that you may be able to make in the introduction or body of your talk.

Now, on occasion you will have a bit more time to prepare. Something in the environment will provide the perfect reference. The Holy Spirit shows us how this is so by the way in which Paul was able to use the altar to the unknown god in his sermon to the Council of the Areopagus in Athens. Timely, appropriate, and lifesaving as this brilliant piece of rhetoric was, it did not simply occur to him out of the blue. His stroll around the city had prepared Paul for that speech. At the time, the altar, doubtless, had made a deep impression upon him. But when he needed a timely remark, the Spirit brought this to mind and used it very appropriately. He had not known at the time when he was seething[1] over it that he would be required to give the Athenian speech.

However, you will know in advance when it is your task to deliver a message. Suppose you have been asked to speak at a banquet. It would be helpful to keep your eyes open when you come into town or when you are being driven to your motel. Look, listen, and talk to the guest who is driving you. Learn all you can in that half hour or so. Something is always there for you to use—if you will only appreciate and appropriate it. Ideas come to the person who is looking for them. In the hour that you have while you are deposited at a motel before you will be picked up to go to dinner, you have ample opportunity to think about what you saw and learned. Use it for that purpose while you are freshening up. Don't turn on the TV and relax. Go to work before you ever arrive at the banquet.

More often, you will be preaching in your own pulpit. Here, the same principles apply. You will, of course, prepare your message beforehand. But when doing so, you probably will want to think illustratively about something that has happened in the community recently (or that was in the news that everyone watches). Something that has occupied the thinking of most of the members of the congregation is excellent illustrative material.[2] Or it may be something that has happened that morning during the hours before church—something someone said,

---

[1] Acts 17:16 indicates that the idolatry in Athens "enraged him."

[2] And sometimes it is essential. If the president dies or if a local school bus overturns, killing several children from your church, you cannot avoid speaking about the matter. The newspapers and the broadcasters will have been stating their views. It will be time for the congregation to hear God's view. Under such all-absorbing conditions, you may even have to change sermons altogether at the last minute. At the very least, you will have to significantly adapt the message that you planned to preach.

something that happened while driving to church, etc. Using illustrative material of this sort usually makes a greater impact than stories that have no immediate relevance to the congregation. In short, matters that relate to the persons to whom you are speaking are always most appropriate. They have a timeliness about them if they are news, if they are comments on news, or if they might become news to those who listen.

There is a timeliness to the use of the Bible as well. In Joshua 1:8, God ordered Joshua not to allow the law to **depart from** [his] **mouth.** What does that mean? There is some debate among the commentators, but at the very least it must mean that he should have the Scriptures available to speak about any and all incidents that occur. That doesn't simply mean having verses to quote in the way that an English curate is often humorously depicted as doing in fiction. What I have in mind is the apt reference to a passage accompanied by timely, appropriate, and applicatory comments. What is in view is ready references to which the preacher may turn to provide helpful commentary that meets a given situation head on. In order to be able to accumulate a wealth of biblical material and to know how to use it in a timely fashion, a preacher must practice doing so in times when others are not.[1] As he reads the newspaper, he should think about what the Bible says, where such biblical data are located, and how they impinge upon the news item that he has just read. The Bible speaks of politics, business, marriage, war, death, interpersonal relations and much more. There is no dearth of biblical information that he may bring to the event. From time to time he might even want to put down the newspaper and look up a verse or two. Then he might wish to study and meditate for half an hour or so about how the two relate.[2] This sort of effort not only will enable him to develop a mentality that relates Scripture to life (a men-

---

[1] If he counsels regularly, he will be better prepared to relate Scripture to a wide variety of unexpected events.
[2] Using commentaries and helps whenever needed.

tality that is a *must* for every preacher), but will also deepen his own spiritual understanding of life[1] (another *must*). As you can see, then, we are talking not merely about how to preach. We are talking as well about how to become a preacher. We are dealing with a preacher's habits, attitudes, mentalities, etc. All those are things that seem to have mattered to the Spirit of God as He inspired the apostles to become the sort of preachers He desired. The right thing at the right time would be incongruous if there was not the right man by whom such messages were delivered.

Paul alluded to this fact in II Corinthians 2:16 when he asked, **"Who is sufficient for these things?"** The word translated **sufficient** (*hikanos*) means "having what it takes to get a job done." He saw himself as totally inadequate to preach the message of life and death (cf. vv. 14-16). But he also recognized that the preaching of the message was vital and that he had been chosen to do it. How were those two facts to be reconciled? He tells us in the next chapter (which is a continuation of the second one): **not because we are self-sufficient, thinking that we could accomplish anything by ourselves, but rather because our sufficiency is from God. He has made us sufficient (*hikanos*) ministers of a new covenant, not of the letter but of the Spirit** (II Corinthians 3:5, 6). There you have it. He was being **transformed into the likeness of the Lord from glory to glory, as from the Lord the Spirit** (v. 18). The Spirit transformed the preacher as well as his preaching. Indeed, his preaching was influenced by this personal transformation.

In our day, apart from an inner work of the Spirit through His Word, no man will preach well. Timeliness, like the other three concerns of the Spirit, is divinely influenced by how much a

---

[1] In Athens, Paul was no tourist. His interest was not in the beauty of the buildings or in the artistry of the sculptors like Phidias. What he saw in the Parthenon, the winged Athena, etc., was gross idolatry. He was impressed with the utter ignorance of all that matters in this, the supposed intellectual center of the world! His attitude toward what he saw was biblical.

preacher develops his own life. So while today the Spirit uses the Word to do gradually for us what he did instantaneously for the apostles, the same *sort* of thing (it won't be infallible as it was in them) is still essential. Is the Spirit, Who is the present Counselor in Whom the Lord Jesus is at work, making you *hikanos*? That is the vital question behind all the others.

Preachers such as Joshua had the Word of God ready to proclaim in a timely fashion whenever it was needed. To do so, he had to constantly **meditate** on the law of the Lord, rehearsing its truths over and over again as they applied to life being lived all around (and within) him. By doing so, he would be *ready* to proclaim it in timely fashion as needed. What a difference a host of men from God like Joshua and Paul would make in our pulpits today! Will you be one of the first of such a new breed?

Chapter 10

How to Be Timely

I have already discussed some of the principles involved in and given some preliminary helps for making a difference in your preaching. Now, I will set forth some additional helps in the form of a program by which you may begin to improve your ability to bring timeliness into your messages. Below I have set forth a number of scenarios that call for some measure of timeliness. They may be used to test your present ability to strike a timely note and to give you some practice at doing so. Most of them call for a limited time to respond. If you observe the time limits carefully, it will help you. The amounts of time in some cases may seem too long since you have other things to do as well; but don't let that disturb you. The actual, real-life situations probably also require thinking while doing other things. I suggest, therefore, that you be honest about the time involved. Don't cheat on the amount of time you devote to preparation; you'll only be cheating yourself if you do. If you cannot come up with a proper answer in the time allotted, chalk that up to the fact that you need to do more work in that area. Then try again a couple of weeks later. You might also think up some new scenarios of your own and, having used these to begin, continue to work on the new ones until you have become proficient at giving timely responses.

On separate paper, succinctly write out what you would say in each of these scenarios.

1. On the way to church you pass a billboard that reads:

> **After 50 years**
> Smith's furniture store
> is going out of business.
> Great reductions!
> All sales final!

You are preaching from Revelation 2:1-7 in an hour and a half. You have twenty minutes before you arrive at the church. Would you refer to this sign? If so, how?

2. The driver who picked you up at the airport tells you that there has been a terrible apartment fire in town in which 9 children and 23 adults have been burned to death. You are to speak at a conference on discipleship. You wonder if there is there some way of relating this occurrence, which probably is in the minds of many persons who will be in the audience, to your subject? There is one hour left before you will speak.

3. At a banquet where you are the principal speaker, a waiter drops a full tray of food and dishes. It causes quite a stir. Can you refer to this incident without further embarrassing him or your hosts? You have about ten minutes to prepare.

4. It is 8 PM Saturday night when you receive the call. One of your elders and his wife have been brutally murdered. The murderer escaped. The motive is unknown. Your message for tomorrow morning on love has been completed for two days. You cannot ignore this tragedy. What will you do or say?

5. At a young married couples' retreat where you are expected to make some brief remarks, the person introducing you talks about how your marriage has been an example and an inspiration to everyone. He goes on and on in an embarrassing fashion that is far wide of the facts. You wonder what to do about it—you have 1 1/2 minutes to determine what to say.

6. During your routine fifteen-minute trip to church in the morning, so far as you can tell nothing worthy of note has happened. So you wonder if you have anything other than the idea of routineness to mention in your sermon on giving. But what could you say—and how? You have about one half hour to decide.

7. You have just been introduced by someone whose introduction, whether intended or not, sounded like an insult: "We are glad to have the Rev. Joe Doakes here today since we couldn't get any of the other speakers that we wanted." The congregation is obviously embarrassed, holding its collective breath to hear what you will say as you rise to speak (1/2 minute).

8. You are to speak at the funeral of a young man who committed suicide. He was not a member of your church. You have three days to prepare.

9. Your message this evening is about the care and discipline afforded by Christ's church. In the afternoon a plane crashes in which the governor and his wife and children, as well as several senators, are killed. It is three hours until the evening message.

10. You are the third of four speakers at a conference. The speaker immediately before you has strongly advocated ordaining women to the pastoral ministry. What will you do or say, if anything? (You have 20 minutes to decide what to do and say).

11. At a Sunday School convention you are the main after-lunch speaker. You have been allotted "no more than twenty-five minutes," the invitation to speak stressed. But after solos, announcements, and so on, that preceded, along with a five minute introduction, you see by the clock that there are but four minutes left of the twenty-five you were allotted! If you speak beyond the allotted time, you will upset the schedule for the thirty workshops to follow. What will you say and do? You have less than a minute to decide—time is of the essence!

12. You are a Calvinist. A previous speaker has taken several pot shots at John Calvin, totally misrepresenting his views. He has also identified you by name with these erroneous views. You are the next speaker on the agenda. Your announced topic is "Modern Cults You Should Know About." Will you respond? If so, how? You have twelve minutes.

13. There has been very little rain in your farming community for a month and a half. The farmers in your congregation have been faced with a crippling drought. Now, for the last four days it hasn't stopped raining as hard as you have ever seen it rain. The farmers are now expressing their fears about flooding, gully-washers, etc., that they say will do every bit as much harm. You had prayed for rain. It has come. What will you say to the congregation this week?

14. In a congregational meeting a member rises and asks for the floor. He publicly accuses you of adultery. He offers no testimony or evidence, and you know that the charge is completely unfounded. What will you do? You have two minutes.

15. In the middle of your sermon on responsibility the door of the church bursts open: a drunk holding an apple enters prattling on unintelligibly about Adam and Eve. He heads for the pulpit. Half way down the aisle he throws the apple at you. You catch it. He then yells out, "Well, what do you have to say about that?" Well, what *do* you have to say?

16. You read, "If anyone knows any reason why this couple may not be lawfully wedded, let him speak now or forever after hold his peace." Immediately a woman you have never seen before rises in her place and says, "I do." What will you do and say next?

17. Your sermon this morning is about witnessing, but it lacks a powerful conclusion. On the way to church you pass a four car wreck from which two ambulances are pulling away. Can you think of how you might use this incident? (You have fifteen minutes).

18. In passing the ladies' room at church on your way to the pulpit you hear a very loud argument taking place. You can't enter, obviously, but you might be able to incorporate some help into your message on reconciliation (you have twenty minutes).

19. The phone call comes as a shocker. Another member has been drawn away into a local cult. This is the fourth family that you have lost to this group which holds doctrines that are akin to those of the Jehovah's Witnesses. Is it time to deal with this matter? If so, how?

20. How should you respond to the profuse "antifundamentalist" propaganda that your community has been subjected to by the liberals who control all of the media in the area? You are a conservative, Bible-believing pastor, and your congregation is in no way associated with radicalism. Yet, more and more, you are lumped together in the minds of the community with the crazies with whom you have no association. What will you do and say?

Well, there you have it. I hope that you do well in answering these twenty scenarios. Think seriously about how to respond. You may never face exactly the same situations, but stirring your brain to think in these ways will assist you when you meet some similar occurrence. Work on it so that in the crunch you will be able to uphold the faith and honor the Lord Jesus Christ. He always knew how to answer everyone. Indeed, the very best model to study in this regard is Christ speaking with the scribes and Pharisees. The apostles' off-the-Spirit's-cuff responses in Acts also afford help.

After you have worked with each of these twenty scenarios to your satisfaction, why not envision at least twenty more of your own (complete with realistic time allotments)? Write them down briefly, as I have in this book, and then come up with your best responses.

Perhaps, if you are close to other pastors, you might together agree to do as follows:

1. Each write in responses to the twenty scenarios in this book, then meet a couple of times to discuss your answers. Add to your own those responses of other pastors that you consider the most useful.

2. Each exchange your own scenarios and then meet to discuss the responses.

3. Think through and discuss the principles that are involved in each good response. List these for future use.[1] Keep a growing list of such principles as from time to time you add to them.
Working with other pastors (or with your elders) in this way will help structure your own efforts so that you will take the work more seriously. This is important to do, especially if you are one whose intentions are good but who has difficulty in following through.

---

[1] For instance, one principle might be: Respond to questions with questions, as Jesus did.

Chapter 11
Putting It All Together

Sermons come as whole packages. Content, language, manner and timeliness are all woven together. In the delivery, the various parts are not discernible—when one preaches well. It is, for instance, precisely when the language protrudes or calls attention to itself that everyone senses something is wrong. The language should serve the content, not the other way around. It should have no life of its own. Moreover, when the manner in which one presents his material is dominant, then, too, something is wrong. Manner should enable the *message* to get through to a particular group of persons. If the note of timeliness becomes so prominent that people can think about nothing else then, again, the preacher has failed. The four elements with which the Holy Spirit is concerned ought to so blend that none of them predominates. In other words, what should be proclaimed is the truth that God wants delivered; nothing should detract from that.

It is when a preacher stumbles for the next word, is obviously embarrassed about how to proceed, or something of the sort that the congregation begins to focus on him rather than the message from God that he is attempting to proclaim. When he uses language that is ungrammatical or inappropriately out of place, people start thinking about how the message is being delivered rather than the message itself. In other words, the four elements we have been discussing can be thought of analytically, can be worked on separately, ought to be improved individually; but when they are in place *in a sermon* they should be fitted tightly together. They belong together, functioning together; there is something wrong when they do not fit together.

Think of an automobile. The fuel system and the electrical systems are separate entities. But for the automobile to function as it was intended, the two must work together. When the battery goes dead, no matter how well the other systems function, the car will not move. If they both are working well, but the brakes have worn, the automobile is likely to be involved in an accident at the next sudden stop—this will influence all parts of the car. If you will, change the metaphor to Paul's use of the body. Each part serves a function that influences the rest of the parts. That is how it is in preaching.

It is wrong for you to think that just because your vocabulary is outstanding, or your content is meaty you can make it on that one element alone. Indeed, if the other three elements fail to measure up to your language or exegetical abilities, then because of the inequality your language or teaching *will* stand out and call attention to itself. The same is true of the other elements.[1] I urge you, therefore, to seek to excel not merely in one or two or even three of these concerns of the Spirit, but in all four. And, as you do, make sure that you know how to combine them in such a way that means none of them dominates to the detriment of the others.

Of course, as this book comes into your hands, you may already excel in one or more of the four elements. That means that your emphasis must be upon the others. Yet in seeking to improve, be careful not to neglect any one of the items since it is altogether possible that an overemphasis on the faulty area will begin to show. As you work to improve any one of them, keep

---

[1] "Our preacher has such a wonderful manner about him, you just want to come to church. But I wish he had something more to say than he does." That is how one person may express the imbalance of manner over against content. Another might say, "You know, he is ever fresh and timely. He knows all about the latest events, uses all the most recent slang. The trouble is, no one gets much out of his messages." These are the kinds of comments that might be forthcoming from parishioners whose preacher hasn't got it all together.

thinking about all four elements. Keep asking yourself, "Now, how does what I am doing fit in with the other concerns of the Spirit?" Never work on one element alone. Keep making improvements across the board. Make sure that you achieve balance.[1]

Sometimes it is difficult to determine exactly which of the elements needs the most effort. How may a preacher know what to work on? Often the school marms will let you know about language. From time to time people will question what you said, "I didn't understand, pastor." It may be their fault that they failed to get what you were driving at. But consider: could it be because you didn't have a clear idea of the message yourself? It should be obvious that you can't deliver a message you don't thoroughly comprehend. So, you may need to work on your exegesis. You may get wind of complaints about your gruffness or, on the contrary, about your lack of courage. Probably, if you do, these will come mostly from your wife or close friends. Do you need to think about the manner in which you approach the congregation? Then, too, you yourself may be aware of the staleness, the sameness, the monotony with which you preach. You are getting tired of thinking, "Here goes another one, just like the other one." If preaching is growing old for you, that is probably a sign that your preaching lacks the note of timeliness. You will have to do something about it.

In all of these, and dozens of other ways, you may become conscious of the lacks in your preaching that need to be addressed. Keep your ears open. If there is an element of arrogance and pride in you that blinds you to what others say—or even to your own suspicions about your preaching—you need to repent of this. You will never grow unless you are teachable. You will not improve unless you develop a self-critical attitude.

---

[1] Because of sin we all tend to become unbalanced; so carefully guard against the tendency.

A self-critical attitude is what you see in Paul in II Corinthians 3:5, where he freely admits that he is not sufficient (*hikanos*) himself, and that his achievements are purely the work of the Holy Spirit. While you do not have the inspiration of the Spirit to enable you to preach as he did; nevertheless, you are fully dependent on the Spirit. It is He Who provided the message, He Who gave you the life, calling, opportunity and gifts to proclaim it. It is He Who molds and sanctifies you to make you fit to address God's people. It is He Who illumines you to understand the Scriptures. It is He Who enables you to improve your preaching. On and on we could go. In the final analysis, all preaching that honors God and blesses His people is the product of the Spirit. There is no place for personal pride—only for gratitude (cf. II Corinthians 4:1).

So, preacher, ask yourself, "Am I **competent to teach others**?" (II Timothy 2:2). Ask also, "Is my **progress apparent to everybody**?" (I Timothy 4:15). If not, obviously you need to do something about it. I am concerned about this matter—concerned enough to make the effort to write about it—for two reasons. First and foremost is concern for the work of the Lord. His message ought to be proclaimed powerfully and effectively. The nature of what He is saying to the world and to the church is so vital and so wonderful, that it deserves nothing less than our best. But I am also interested because some day you may be preaching to my children—or grandchildren. That is one reason why Paul says that progress should be apparent to all; all of us have a stake in it!

If you find that you are not able to improve in one or more of the four areas about which the Spirit expressed His concern, I suggest two things. First, pray about it. If the Spirit is concerned, and if He helps us in our infirmities, you can be sure that He will take a personal interest. Second, find help somewhere. Read books, talk to other preachers, take a refresher course at a seminary. But do *something. Don't give up.* Keep at it until you begin to change and are able to show real **progress**. That is what God desires. A preacher who is satisfied with what he is capable of doing is not progressing. Nor is he even able to remain at whatever level he has attained. He is drifting backward. The nature of the task is such that one must always be growing, always progressing. And whenever one is making headway, it is always against the stream. The world, the flesh, and the devil are all opposed to good preaching. Your own remaining, sinful proclivities stand in the way. The appeal of other things tends to draw you away from the task. Among all the sinful problems that preachers have, perhaps laziness and pride head the list. Watch out for these. Keep asking God to remove them. Fight against them. Cultivate diligence and humility instead. These attitudes are crucial to the progress that is necessary in achieving the proper fit between the right message, in the right language, presented in the right manner, at the right time.

Chapter 12

Conclusion

I've often heard people joke about it, but this past year was the first time that I actually ran into anyone to whom it was a serious matter. I'm talking about the idea that there is no need for a preacher today to prepare his sermons. The not-very-good joke goes something like this:

> Joe: "I don't prepare my messages."
>
> Bill: "You don't?"
>
> Joe: "No, I just let the Spirit move me when I get up to preach."
>
> Bill (talking to himself under his breath): "There must be something wrong there. The Spirit couldn't have moved him to preach a sermon as bad as that."

Or, in another version:

> Joe: "I never prepare my sermons ahead of time."
>
> Bill: "Sure sounds like it!"

This year I was speaking to a preacher who told me that the denomination to which he belongs used to look down on any sort of prior preparation. Preparation was supposed to quench the Spirit. The idea was that the Lord Himself would preach through a Spirit-filled preacher. So the only preparation necessary was the preparation of the preacher, not his message. Now, there is nothing wrong with the preacher preparing himself before the Lord. Indeed, that is good and necessary. But to arrogate to one's self the passages that we have been looking at reflects the worst sort of exegesis. The preaching of the apostles was unique. And that is true because God promised inspiration to them. He has made no such promise to you or me.

The preacher who told me about his denomination was thankful that the trend has changed. Through more careful exegesis of the Scriptures, many men now see that they are required to grow not only personally, but also in their ability to communicate God's Word.

Let's face it. You *aren't* inspired. Therefore, you must work at improving your preaching. Certainly, as you understand more and more of what the Bible teaches about preaching and assimilate that material into your preaching, the Spirit (Who works through His Word) will enable you to become more and more effective. Your preaching to some extent, however small that may be, will begin to approximate the preaching of the apostles. But, of course, it will always remain inferior to their inspired preaching. Just as all true Christians aim at perfection, knowing that they will never reach it in this life, so too do preachers emulate inspired preaching, knowing they shall never attain to it either. Why? You rarely rise as high as your goal. If your goal is low, you will probably not reach it; you will settle for some quite inferior sort of preaching. If it is very high, though you won't reach it, you will rise higher than if your goal was low. You won't ever settle for mediocre preaching.

So, as Jesus noted, there was no need for the apostles to prepare beforehand what they would say. The reason He mentioned this is because preparation is normal and proper. He was going to do something quite out of the ordinary for the apostles that would preclude the normal process of preparing to speak. He would give them instant messages, as the Spirit took control of them and they spoke His truth in His words. There was no need for preparation. Since we have no such promise, there is every need to do what Jesus told the apostles *not* to do: we *must* prepare beforehand.

We must **practice** (as He also mentioned) what we are going to say, the language in which we shall say it, the wisest manner in which to say it, and how we might respond in timely ways to the situation in which we say it. Let's talk a bit about the idea of practicing. The verb used in Luke 21:14 is *promelatao* which means to practice beforehand. The verb *melatao* means to practice. Add the *pro* to it, and it has the idea of doing so ahead of time. Clearly, the method to which Jesus referred requires some sort of rehearsal of what one will say in a given circumstance. Whether he rehearses as Demosthenes did, shouting to the waves with marbles in his mouth, or simply rehearses his message in his study, some sort of practice like this is necessary for most inexperienced preachers. Probably, the best way for them to do so is to go into the church alone and actually deliver the message behind their pulpits.[1] Others, with a good bit more experience, will still find themselves repeating certain portions of their message under their breath as they drive along in their cars or lie in bed at night. However, you do it,[2] the point is to *do it*!

What is the incentive for improvement in preaching? Is it the approval of your people? Well, that's not a bad thing if it means that they will more willingly hear God's Word and live it. Is it the impact that your preaching will make in a world that is rapidly propelling itself toward devastation? Certainly effective preaching is the only true remedy for the problem. Is it so that your children and grandchildren may hear the truth in ways that will guide and direct them in the ways they should go? Absolutely. But none of these incentives is the great one.

Listen to the apostle Paul writing to Timothy: **Do your best to present yourself to God tried and true, a workman who won't be ashamed, cutting the Word of truth with accuracy** (II Timothy 2:15). That is the great incentive for improvement.

---

[1] Possibly, at times, more than once. But one must be careful not to muddy the canvas.

[2] Working through scenarios, as I suggest, is another way to practice.

Some day, when you stand before the Lord and answer not only for how you lived your personal life, but also for how you proclaimed the Scriptures in your role as a teaching elder of His church, will you be praised or ashamed? Think about that. Make some decisions today to begin improving your preaching. And stick to them. If you do, and if you develop and use the gifts that have been granted to you as He expects you to, on that all-important day when everything else seems insignificant, you will hear Him say, "Well done, you good and faithful servant." In that hour, you will see that all the practice, all the effort, all the time spent was surely worth it. My hope is that this book will in some small measure play a part in bringing about that happy event.